LIGHTHOUSES of the World

LIGHTHOUSES
of the World

Compiled by the International Association of Marine Aids to Navigation
and Lighthouse Authorities

The
Globe
Pequot
Press

Old Saybrook, Connecticut

Preface

For the navigator, lighthouses, whether simple wood fires lit on top of a rocky peak or tall towers with sophisticated optics, have always been indispensable references along coastlines — a reference as well as a symbol of help provided by men of the land to men of the sea.

Their rays of light appear so solitary when we observe lighthouses from land. For the mariner to distinguish and recognize individual lighthouses, it is necessary for them to stand on the bridge of a ship at night to see the long or short light flashes silently communicating with them. These beams stretch beyond borders to weave a thread of light that has neither beginning nor end.

Each country's coastline has contributed to the network within the bounds of its own resources and ability, for the same goal: the safety of the mariner.

Without doubt, other techniques play a part in safe navigation. The modern mariner uses many tools to plot his course. Nevertheless, lighthouses maintain their symbolic value.

As a link between land and sea, lighthouses symbolize the courage and often prowess of builders; they are part and parcel of the history of each region of the world.

Today, most of these "sentries of the sea" no longer need a keeper to light and look after them. A page of history has been turned for these voluntary exiles that for centuries have kept watch on sheer coastlines where the rocks are battered by the waves and the wind. Some lights have finally been extinguished, their towers and keepers' cottages abandoned, for the lack of sufficient means to maintain them. Their optics also, works of talented designers, sometimes true masterpieces, are dismantled and removed from all memory. Other equipment, just as precious, disappears purely and simply.

Many administrators of maritime countries, aware of the value of these monuments as witnesses to history, have been moved by this situation and are now looking into ways of preserving them.

The International Association of Lighthouse Authorities (IALA), in order to address the need expressed by many maritime administrations, has created a panel commissioned to study the challenges of protecting these buildings and to propose solutions. The panel believes it is important to gain the public's attention with regard to this unrecognized and therefore threatened aspect of world heritage.

This book, by introducing lighthouses to the general public, is a small stone in the preservation of a heritage completely devoted to safety. It is one of the fruits of the work and spirit of cooperation that has inspired all members of the association.

JEAN-MARIE CALBET President of the Consultative Committee of IALA concerning
lighthouses and aids to navigation of historic interest
ROBERT J. KINGSTON President of IALA
TORSTEN KRUUSE Secretary General of IALA

From the First Lights to the Satellites

COAL LIGHT

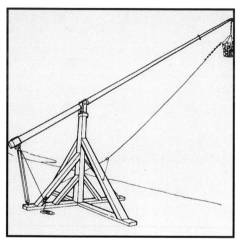

SWAP LIGHT

CORDOUAN LIGHTHOUSE

The first known aids to navigation were lighthouses. Some of them are famous but cannot be traced in history (Alexandia, Ostia, Rhodes, etc.).

During the Roman period, masonry towers were built and some of them still exist (Dover Castle). After the destruction of the Roman Empire, the monks took over the job and lit fires on the top of some church towers to serve as navigational aids (St. Catherine, the Tour de la Lanterne at La Rochelle in France, Venedig in Germany).

Other devices were then used in the 16th and 17th centuries. Some of them were very simple, but others were already more sophisticated (Cordouan).

Until the 19th century the "Lights of the Sea" remained simple wood or coal fires in the open air sometimes sheltered from the weather as they were in the old abbeys, but with no device for improving the light intensity.

From the First Lights to the Satellites

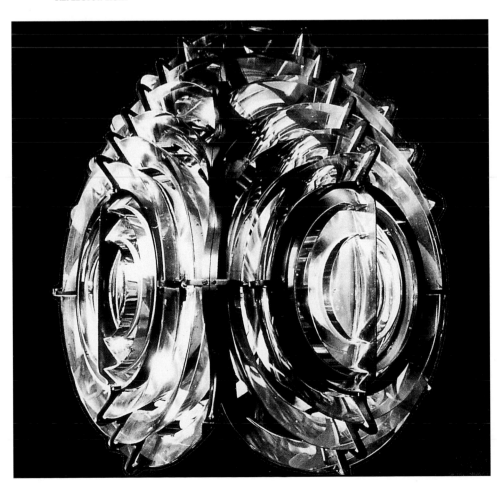

At the time of the Industrial Revolution the real lighthouses appeared. They took advantage of the new technologies in civil engineering and in physics, which led to reflector lights and then the Fresnel lenses.

New power sources (oil, gas, electricity, and later solar and wind energy) allowed stable lights to be obtained. These new power sources also permitted the diversification of aids to navigation — lighted buoys and beacons, lightships — before satellites appeared.

REFLECTOR LIGHT

FIRST LENS APPARATUS
LOT ORDER
CORDOUAN 1823

Is IALA Useful?

LANBY ON THE WESER

The development of maritime vessels and the quickly developing techniques in the field of aids to navigation made it necessary to create a permanent international organization that would be responsible for centralizing studies and research and would become a forum for the lighthouse authorities of various countries to exchange information and ideas.

The 1955 Scheveningen Lighthouse Conference resulted in IALA being created 2 years later, in 1957.

Because IALA is a nongovernmental organization, it needs the support of intergovernmental organizations, sometimes U.N. bodies (ITU, IMO, etc.), to have its recommendations recognized and implemented by governments.

IALA's present structure and organization are shown in the opposite figure.

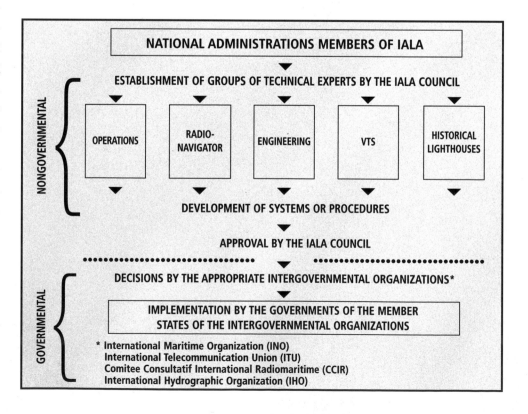

NATIONAL ADMINISTRATIONS MEMBERS OF IALA

ESTABLISHMENT OF GROUPS OF TECHNICAL EXPERTS BY THE IALA COUNCIL

NONGOVERNMENTAL

| OPERATIONS | RADIO-NAVIGATOR | ENGINEERING | VTS | HISTORICAL LIGHTHOUSES |

DEVELOPMENT OF SYSTEMS OR PROCEDURES

APPROVAL BY THE IALA COUNCIL

DECISIONS BY THE APPROPRIATE INTERGOVERNMENTAL ORGANIZATIONS*

GOVERNMENTAL

IMPLEMENTATION BY THE GOVERNMENTS OF THE MEMBER STATES OF THE INTERGOVERNMENTAL ORGANIZATIONS

* International Maritime Organization (INO)
International Telecommunication Union (ITU)
Comitee Consultatif International Radiomaritime (CCIR)
International Hydrographic Organization (IHO)

Is IALA Useful?

THE *SIR WILLIAM ALEXANDER* (CANADA)
IN THE ICE

I ALA now also considers improving traffic management in straits, waterways, and port approaches. These studies are made in cooperation with other international organizations representing the various activi-

UNMANNED LIGHTVESSEL

ties concerned (port authorities, shipmasters, pilots, shipowners).

The adoption of the "Guidelines for Vessel Traffic Services" by IMO in 1986 and the publication of "The IALA, IAPH, IMPA World VTS Guide" can be considered as the first results of these studies.

Is IALA Useful?

When IALA was created in 1957 it consisted of 20 members. Now it gathers together 80 countries worldwide. The first components of IALA were nations' maritime administrations, but now they are joined by equipment manufacturers and consultants. Together they are studying the numerous problems encountered by aids to navigation authorities every day.

BUOYS OF THE MARITIME
BUOYAGE SYSTEM

In 1971 the development of a uniform international maritime buoyage system became the priority of IALA. At that time, a series of wrecks in the Dover Strait led 51 mariners to death. It appeared that the deaths had been caused by a misunderstanding of the buoyage in the area.

BEACON CARRYING
A MARKING LIGHT
AND A RACON

An international agreement on the new system called The IALA International Maritime Buoyage System was signed in 1982. It had not been possible, however, to achieve a totally uniform system. As a result the seas are now divided into 2 regions — A and B — where the same rules apply but with reversed colors on lateral marks.

Conception and setting up of the new system led IALA to enhance technical cooperation between developed and developing countries.

PORKKALA LIGHTHOUSE, FINLAND

Marking for the Future

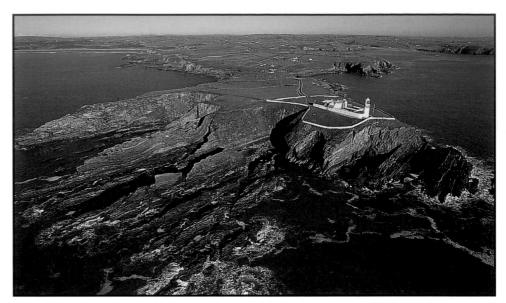

GALLEY HEAD LIGHTHOUSE, IRELAND

VESSEL TRAFFIC SERVICE

IALA continues to extend its studies in the field of Vessel Traffic Services. The trend is to have more standardization (liability, training of personnel, uniform procedures) so that ships follow the rules to expedite traffic, particularly where there are navigational or environmental concerns. The protection of the maritime environment and the prevention of collisions at sea depend heavily on such rules.

Another important task given to IALA by IMO is the development of a worldwide radio-navigation system. IALA has already declared that it is in favor of having a civilian terrestrial radio-navigation system, managed at an international level and operated as a backup for the satellite system. These two systems, American and Russian, have already started to work jointly.

JAAKO LIGHTHOUSE, FINLAND

Marking
for the
Future

I t is becoming more and more evi-
dent that the future will not see
some of the present systems in
use or take precedence over all
the others. On the contrary, studies in
progress show that each system (traditional seamarks, terrestrial or satellite
navigation, VTS) will have a role to
serve. Each system will evolve to play a
role in an interactive group of aids to
navigation where each will play its own
part in the function of others.

GLOBAL POSITIONING SYSTEM (GPS)

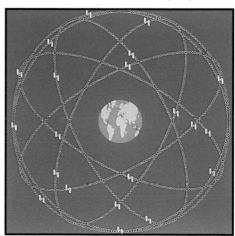

PIERRES NOIRES LIGHTHOUSE, FRANCE

AFR

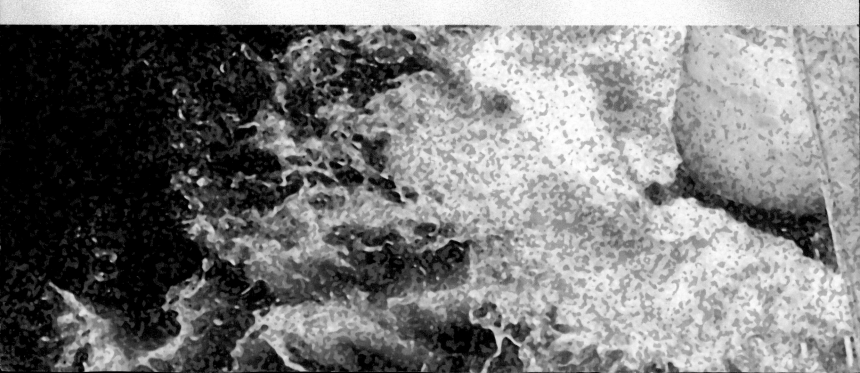

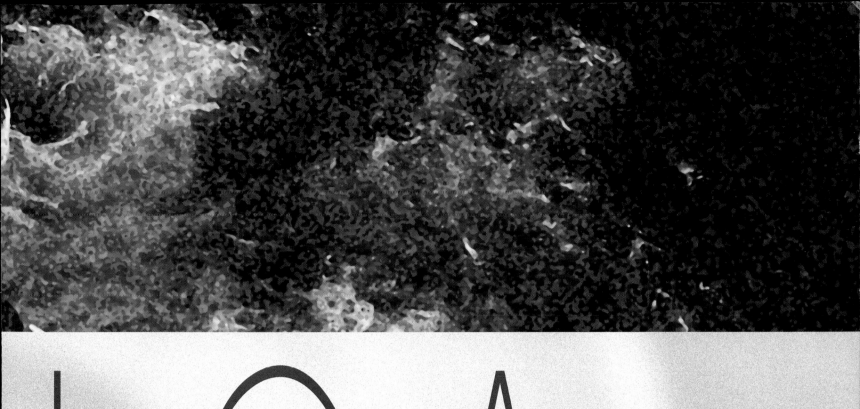

ICA

South Africa

The History of the South African Lighthouse Service

The foundation for a Lighthouse Service in South Africa was laid on April 12, 1824, when the first solidly constructed lighthouse was commissioned at Green Point in the Cape. At the time of Union in 1910, the lighthouse departments of both the Colonial Governments of the Cape and Natal were absorbed by the South African Railways and Harbours (SAR&H) and administered by a Lighthouse Engineer from Johannesburg. Statutory authority for the control of the Lighthouse Service was transferred by Act. No. 22 of 1916 to the Rail Administration.

When the South African Transport Services (old SAR&H) became a commercialized company in April 1990 by means of the Legal Succession to the South African Transport Services Act, Act No. 9 of 1989, statutory authority ". . . to erect, maintain and operate lighthouses, beacons, port lights and signal stations . . ." was granted to Transnet. The Lighthouse Service became the responsibility of Portnet, a division of Transnet, with Portnet being responsible for all major ports.

During 1992, the head office of the Lighthouse Service was relocated from Johannesburg to Cape Town as a self-supporting business unit of Portnet and is now accommodated in the Green Point Lighthouse complex.

Portnet Lighthouse Services, with a staff complement of 155, is responsible for all the lighthouses and beacons along the South African coast. It is also responsible, under contract, for the Aids to Navigation in the eight Portnet ports, all the Sea Fisheries harbors, and most of the other privately owned harbors and marinas.

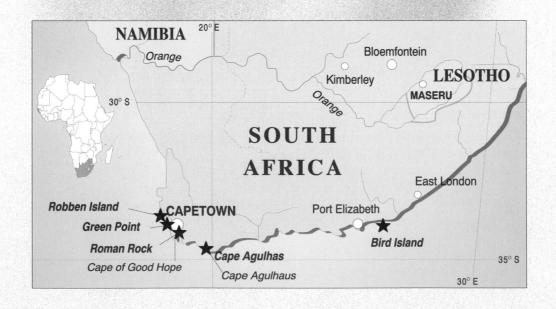

ROBBEN ISLAND LIGHTHOUSE

Geographical Position:
Latitude 33°48'52" S
Longitude 18°22'29" E
Table Bay in the South Atlantic Ocean
Commissioned: April 1864
Architect/Builder: John Scott
Tucker/Joseph Flack
Construction Material: Rubble masonry
Tower Height: 15 meters
Focal Plane Height: 47 meters

General: The lighthouse is situated on the highest point of the island. Over the years the island has been used as a leper colony, naval base, and prison. During 1885 the colonial government enacted a bill declaring consent for the construction of the lighthouse and the collection of light dues. This bill set the precedent for the collection of the light dues in respect of all lighthouses in South Africa.

The lighthouse and the island were declared a National Monument and a World Heritage Site during 1996.

Description: The lighthouse tower is circular in form and built of rubble masonry, which was quarried on the island, except for the top layers of granite.

The original first-order fixed lens is still in use, but an electrical supply is now provided by the island authorities and powers a 1.5 kw lamp. The optic produces an occulting white light of 174,000 candelas with a red sector covering the notorious Whale Rock.

CAPE AGULHAS LIGHTHOUSE

Geographical Position:
Latitude 34°49'42" S
Longitude 20°00'33" E
Southernmost point of Africa
Commissioned: March 1849
Architect/Builder: Lt. Col. C. C. Mitchell/ Mr. William Martin
Construction Material: Limestone
Tower Height: 27 meters
Focal Plane Height: 31 meters

General: This lighthouse is situated close to the southernmost point of Africa. It also accommodates the only Lighthouse Museum in Southern Africa.

The design of this lighthouse was inspired by the Pharos of Alexandria, and the original living quarters are attached to both sides of the main tower with a small false tower at either end. These small towers served as chimneys for the fireplaces in the main rooms of these dwellings.

This lighthouse was declared a National Monument on March 2, 1973.

Description: A 27 meter round masonry tower, painted white with red horizontal bands, supports a lantern house and a first-order revolving optic, consisting of four catadioptric lens panels. The optic produces a flash of 7,500,000 candelas every 2 seconds and has a focal height of 31 meters. Electricity is supplied by the national network with a standby diesel/alternator plant and it is also equipped with a radio beacon. This lighthouse is manned by a Senior Lightkeeper.

GREEN POINT LIGHTHOUSE (CAPE)

Geographical Position:
Latitude 33°54'04" S
Longitude 18°24'02" E
South Atlantic Ocean
Commissioned: April 1824
Architect/Builder: Herman Shutte
Construction Material: Stone rubble
Tower Height: 16 meters
Focal Plane Height: 20 meters

General: This is the oldest solidly constructed lighthouse on the South African coastline. It also accommodates the Head Office of the Lighthouse Service.
This lighthouse was declared a National Monument on January 12, 1973.

Description: A 16 meter square masonry tower, painted white with diagonal red bands, supports a white lantern house with a third-order revolving optic with 3 equally spaced catadioptric lens panels. The optic produces a flash of 850,000 candelas every 10 seconds and has a focal height of 20 meters.
Electricity is supplied by the national electricity network with a standby diesel/alternator plant. The station also is equipped with a nautophone-type fog signal.

ROMAN ROCK LIGHTHOUSE (CAPE)

Geographical Position:
Latitude 34°10'52" S
Longitude 18°27'39" E
Inside False Bay off the Cape Peninsular
— South Atlantic Ocean
Commissioned: September 1861
Architect/Builder: Alexander
Gordon/Robert Cousins
Construction Material: Cast iron
Tower Height: 14.6 meters
Focal Plane Height: 17 meters

General: This is the only South African lighthouse erected on a rock exposed at low tide and awash almost continuously at high tide. Work commenced on building the lighthouse in 1857 but was not completed until 4 years later. Due to inclement weather and heavy seas only 962 hours of work were possible during this period.

Description: The lighthouse is made of cast iron segments bolted together to form a conical tower 14.6 meters high. The design allowed for the first 3 meters of the tower to be filled with concrete. Before this could be completed, cracks were found in the cast iron plates which required wrought iron hoops to be fitted. As a result a granite wall 1.2 meters wide was built to encase the first 3.8 meters of the tower, which was completed in 1867.

The existing lighting system is comprised of an AGA PRB 24 rotating beacon producing a white flash of 147,000 candelas every 6 seconds within a GRP lantern house.

In 1994 a helicopter landing facility of stainless steel was erected on an adjacent rock with a walkway to the lighthouse. The station is supplied with solar power and is equipped with a racon.

BIRD ISLAND LIGHTHOUSE

Geographical Position:
Latitude 33°50'29" S
Longitude 26°17'13" E
Indian Ocean
Commissioned: May 1873
Architect/Builder: Joseph Flack
(Clerk of Works)
Mr. Godfrey of Cape Town (Builder)
Construction Material: Stone
Tower Height: 26 meters
Focal Plane Height: 30 meters

General: The first structure was erected in 1852. It was made of wood and pyramidal in shape. It exhibited two white lights which, when in line, indicated Doddington Rocks. This was replaced by a masonry structure in 1873, and it exhibited a fixed red light. During 1890, the Lighthouse Commission recommended that the range of the light be increased and that it should have a white flashing character. As a result the tower was raised by 6 meters in 1892 and a new lantern house and optic were obtained from the Chance Brothers. The optic was comprised of a first-order dioptric, double flashing white light every 30 seconds, with a light source being a six-wick Trinity House Douglas burner.

During 1906, communications improved when pigeons were introduced to convey messages between the island and the Port Elizabeth lighthouse. In 1921 a wireless telephone was installed.

Description: The tower is approximately 15 meters high and was built from local stone and granite blocks brought to the island in 1871 and 1873. Single-story accommodation blocks were built on either side of the tower.

The station was automated in 1968 following the installation of 3 diesel alternators and a new optic. The optic now consists of an AGA PR-240 optic comprising 250 mm catadioptric four-panel lens mounted on a pedestal. A 1,500 watt lamp provides the light and the optic produces a double white flash of 1,465 cds every 20 seconds.

Algeria

الديوان الوطني للإشارة البحرية

History

Between 1962 (the year of Algerian independence) and 1971, lighthouses were controlled by a department attached to Central Services called Technical Service of Maritime Signalisation.

In 1971, responsibility changed to that of the Ministry of Public Works, creating the Service of Maritime Signalisation. In 1985, the title of the service was changed to National

Office of Maritime Signalisation under the control of the Ministry of Environmental Development.

It is a public establishment devoted to Aids to Navigation (lighthouses, radio beacons, lighted beacons, floating marks, beacons, DGPS station, etc.) and oceanographic works (wave measurements, wave power, tide data acquisition and underwater services).

It contains three sub-directorates and four regional units.

يوان الوطني

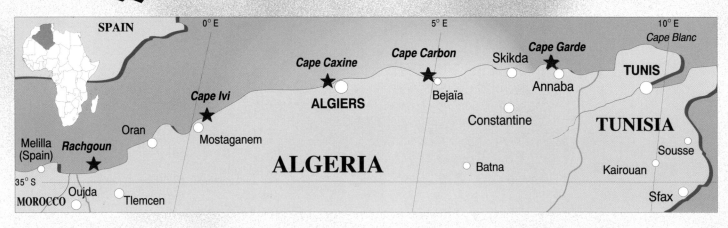

CAPE CARBON LIGHTHOUSE

Geographical Position:
Latitude 36°46'34" N
Longitude 05°06'20" E
Construction period: 1900-1905
Construction Material: Masonry tower and building of smooth dressed stone.

Description: The cylindrical lantern of the lighthouse is supported off a low rectangular building constructed upon a steep rock. The optic consists of four Fresnel panels with a focal length at 700 mm. It is lit with an ordinary 1,000 watt lamp connected to a 220 volt supply.
The lighthouse is situated within a sheltered sea area and has maintained its original appearence but has been automated. Parts of it are open to the public.

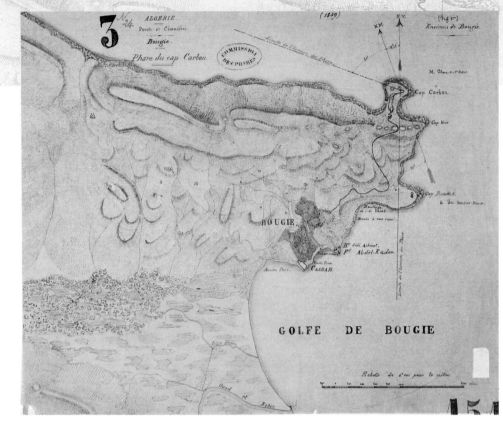

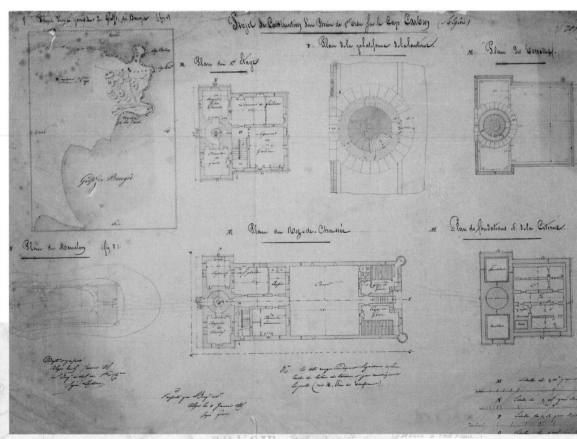

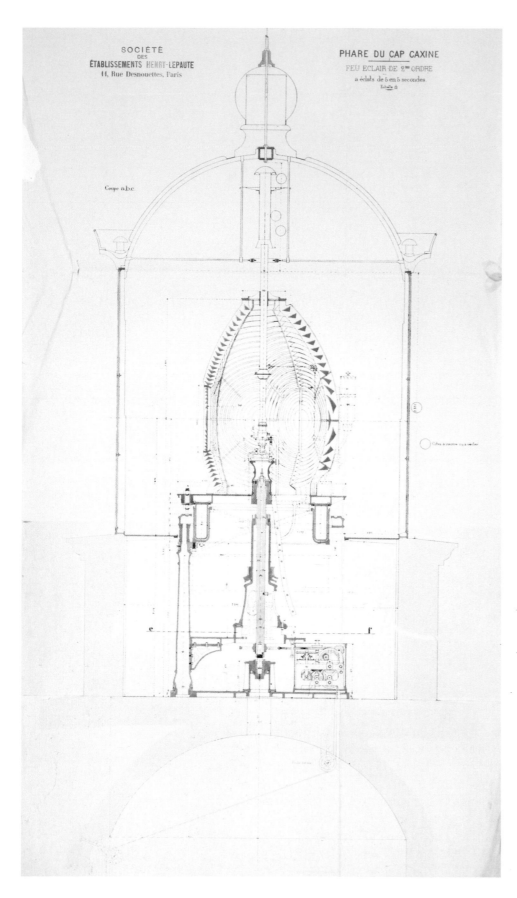

SOCIÉTÉ
DES
ÉTABLISSEMENTS HENRY-LEPAUTE
11, Rue Desnouettes, Paris

PHARE DU CAP CAXINE
FEU ECLAIR DE 2me ORDRE
a éclats de 5 en 5 secondes

Coupe a.b.c

CAPE CAXINE LIGHTHOUSE

Geographical Position:
Latitude 36°49'00" N
Longitude 02°57'00" E
Year of construction: 1868
Construction Material: Masonry tower and building of smooth dressed stone.

Description: The square tower is painted white, supporting a lantern equipped with an optic made up of four Fresnel lenses with a focal length of 700 mm. This optic is lit using a standard 1,000 watt lamp fed from a 220 volt electricity supply.

The lighthouse is situated within a sheltered sea area and parts of it are open to the public.

The lighthouse building has remained unaltered since its construction. Today it is automatic and manned.

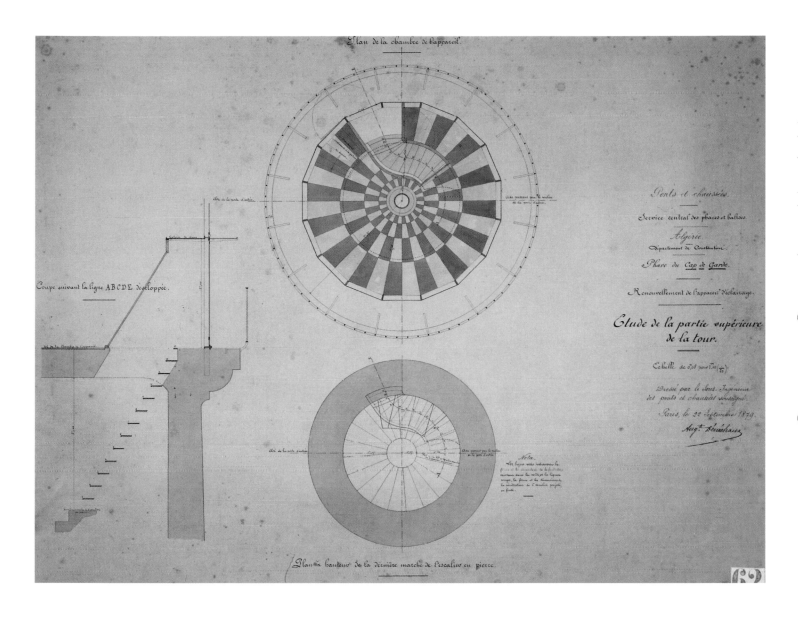

CAPE GARDE LIGHTHOUSE

Geographical Position:
Latitude 36°58'05" N
Longitude 07°47'06" E
Year of construction: 1900
Construction Material: Masonry
tower and building of smooth
dressed stone.

Description: The low square tower is close
to a building painted white and typical of
the local architecture. The cylindrical lantern contains an optic consisting of four
Fresnel lenses each with a focal length of
700 mm. It is lit with a standard 1,000 watt
lamp fed from a 220 volt supply.

The lighthouse is situated within a sheltered
sea area and has retained its original
appearance but today it is automatic.

It is always manned and part of it is open
to the public.

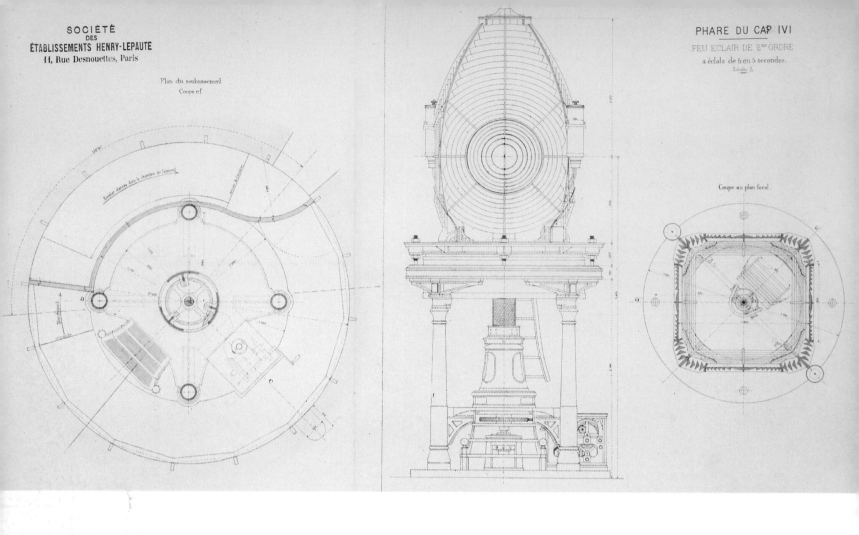

SOCIÉTÉ
DES
ÉTABLISSEMENTS HENRY-LEPAUTE
11, Rue Desnouettes, Paris

PHARE DU CAP IVI
FEU ÉCLAIR DE 2ᵐᵉ ORDRE
à éclats de 5 en 5 secondes.
Échelle ∆

CAPE IVI LIGHTHOUSE

Geographical Position:
Latitude 36°06'50" N
Longitude 00°13'40" E
Construction year: 1898
Construction Material: Masonry tower of dressed stone.

Description: The optic consists of four Fresnel lenses, each having a focal length of 700 mm. It is lit by a standard 1,000 watt lamp fed from a 220 volt supply. The lighthouse is situated within a sheltered sea area and has retained its original appearance.
It is now automatic but is always manned and parts are open to the public.

Cape Ivi lighthouse

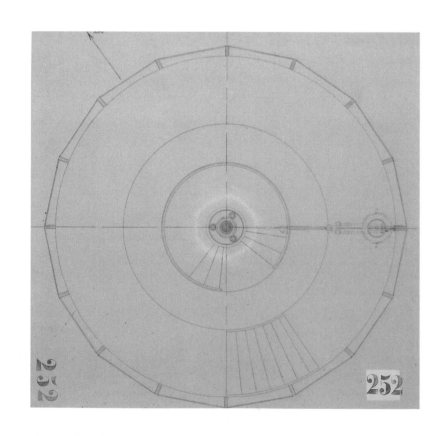

252

RACHGOUN ISLAND LIGHTHOUSE

Geographical Position:
Latitude 35°19'27" N
Longitude 01°28'39" E
Construction year: 1870
Construction Material: Masonry tower of smooth stone with dressed stones used on returns.

Description: The low square tower rises from the middle of one side of the rectangular building.

The whole station contains a number of yards and two other outbuildings, all surrounded by a perimeter wall. The lighthouse lantern contains an optic made up of four Fresnel lenses each with a focal length of 500 mm. It is lit by a standard 75 watt lamp fed from a low voltage, 24 volt supply.
The lighthouse is situated in a sheltered sea area and has maintained its original appearance.

Electrical Supply Service Lighthouse and Beacons

Benin

Electrical Supply Service Lighthouse
and Beacons

The Technical Director of the Port of Cotonou Authority has autonomy over all the functions and infrastructure of the port. This includes responsibility for research, development and the updating and maintenance of Maritime Signalling and Aids to Navigation, within and leading into the port.

The Cotonou Lighthouse, the beacons on either side of the entrance, buoyage, port lights, VTS and the telemetry used to control them are all run by the Electrical Supply Service under the control of the Port Authority.

COTONOU LIGHTHOUSE

Geographical Position:
Latitude 06°21'02" N
Longitude 02°26'04" E
Atlantic Ocean
Light first exhibited: 1928
Construction Material: Steel
Tower Height: 28 meters
Focal Plane Height: 30.97 meters

History: The present Cotonou Lighthouse had its light first exhibited on September 1, 1928, for the purpose of directing ships into the port.

Description: The lighthouse consists of a stayed latice steel tower with a square cross-section of sides 3.8 meters supported off a reinforced concrete raft foundation 8 meters square by 4 meters high.

The main navigation light is provided by a four-panel rotating glass lens optic giving 4 equal flashes. Prior to 1980, the light source was 1,500 watts taken from the station's 3-phase AC supply. After that date the light source was replaced with a 650 watt AC halogen lamp. The emergency light consists of a small four-panel optic fixed directly to the top of the main optic and fitted with a 36 watt lamp. The characters of the main and emergency lights are the same, giving one white flash every 5 seconds. The main light has an intensity of 1,250,000 cd giving a range of 25 nautical miles and the emergency 10 nautical miles.

The optic is rotated by an electrically rewound, falling weight mechanism and floats in a mercury bath. The whole optic is housed in a curved glazed lantern 2 meters in diameter.

The station is powered from the port's electricity supply but should this fail, the main light immediately charges over to the emergency, which is maintained from a 12V 80AH battery supply. If the outage is for an extended period, then the whole station is powered from a 3-phase AC diesel standby alternator.

Senegal

The Lighthouse and Beacons Subdivision of Senegal is managed by the Autonomous Port of Dakar resulting from an agreement with the State of Senegal. Despite a real interest in preservation, Senegal has not yet formulated a policy for safeguarding historic lighthouses.

MAMELLES LIGHTHOUSE

Geographical Position:
Latitude 14°43'4" N
Longitude 17°30'2" W
Atlantic Ocean
Light first exhibited: 1864
Constructor: French Lighthouse Service
Construction Material: Stone

History: Built at the same time as the Port of Dakar, the Mamelles Lighthouse is the first lighthouse to exist in this part of Africa. Its history is closely linked with that of the region and the time of King Cayor.
Located in a governmentally protected area, the lighthouse is open to the public.
Description: The equipment consists of a revolving optic floating in a mercury bath. It has a range of 29 nautical miles and although the station is automated, it remains manned.

CAPE MANUEL LIGHTHOUSE

Geographical Position:
Latitude 14°39' N
Longitude 17°26' W
Atlantic Ocean
Light first exhibited: 1865
Construction Material: Stone and cement, concrete for the tower

History: This lighthouse was constructed from a mixture of concrete, new for its time, and traditional materials in the form of bricks and cement. It is situated within a governmental protected area and is open to the public.

Description: Cape Manuel Lighthouse has a rotating optic floating in a mercury bath and its range is 19 nautical miles. Although the station has been automated, it is still manned by keepers.

GANDIOLE LIGHTHOUSE

Geographical Position:
Latitude 15°53'8" N
Longitude 16°30'6" W
Atlantic Ocean
Light first exhibited: 1836
Constructor : French Lighthouse Service
Construction Material: Concrete

History: The Gandiole Lighthouse was the first seamark built by the French in order to help the ships coming from the ocean and making passage up the Senegal River. It is an old lighthouse and its history is linked with the colonization of the area. It is a listed historic monument and it is open to the public.

Description: The original equipment has been replaced with a modern equivalent and the old one has been kept. The Gandiole Lighthouse is now automated and unmanned. The light has a range of 14 nautical miles.

AME

RICA

Brazil

Admiral Moraes Rego
Aids to Navigation
Center

The Centro de Sinalização Nautica e Reparos Almirante Moraes Rego (CAMR), the Admiral Moraes Rego Aids to Navigation Center, is located on Mocanguê Island, off Niteroi City, in the State of Rio de Janeiro, Brazil.

CAMR is inserted within the chain of command under the Directorate of Hydrography and Navigation (DHN), the Brazilian Navy Hydrographic Office. Founded on January 26, 1876, with the denomination of Repartição de Farois (Lighthouse Bureau), the Center was transferred over to its present headquarters on Mocanguê Island in 1965, and named after Admiral Tacito Reis de Moraes Rego, a celebrated hydrographer.

As directed by DHN, CAMR supervises the establishment and maintenance of all aids to navigation along the 5,000 nautical-mile Brazilian coastline as well as on the numerous and extensive interior waterways. To do its duty, CAMR relies upon the cooperation of six Aids to Navigation Services, which are under the administrative and military jurisdiction of the respective Naval Districts, to act together toward a common end.

SANTO ANTONIO LIGHTHOUSE

Geographical Position:
Latitude 13°00'61" S
Longitude 38°31'97" W
South Atlantic Ocean
Commissioned: Décember 1698
Architect/Builder: Governor Joâo
de Alencastro (Portuguese
Administration)
Construction Material: Stone masonry
Tower Height: 18 meters
Focal Plane Height: 22 meters

General: Built in the first fortress of Brazil, it is the most important historical feature of Salvador City and a tourist point.
It is known as the very first lighthouse on the American continent, and also accommodates a hydrographic museum. Mainly, it is a very important aid to those entering or leaving the Port of Salvador.

Description: A frustum tower with horizontal strips painted white and black, the lighthouse carries a BBT 3500 mm lantern with 1,000 watt, 220 volt halogen lamp, connected to commercial electricity power. The optic produces the following flashes: white (510,000 candelas) and red (204,000 candelas) every 5 seconds.

Canada

Lighthouses and the Canadian Coast Guard

Canadians have been involved with the construction, efficient operation and care of the nation's lighthouses since French-Canadian colonists helped build a lighthouse at Fort Louisbourg in 1733. Over a hundred years before Canada united, Canadian Coast Guard predecessors like Quebec's Trinity House began the awesome task of creating a system of lights to cover thousands of kilometers of Canadian coastline. Colonial leaders quickly realized the need for lighthouses to guide mariners through Canada's many treacherous straits and entrances to harbors. Sambro Island Lighthouse, built in 1758 by colonial Nova Scotia, was the first of hundreds of still-operating lighthouses to be built in Canada. Under intense pressure from Canadian mariners, Canadian colonial governments embarked on a massive lighthouse construction program with the help of British funding in the 1860s. Some of the most impressive and navigationally crucial lighthouses, the renowned Imperial Towers, were built during the decade of Canada's birth and set the stage for the creation of one of the world's most impressive system of lights to this day.

The Canadian Confederation in 1867 combined and strengthened this system of lights when the federal government centralized control of the lighthouses under the Department of Marine and Fisheries. In 1936, the responsibility of caring for the lightstations was delegated to the Department of Transport and its fleet of seagoing vessels. This fleet was renamed the Canadian Coast Guard in 1962. Now amalgamated with the Department of Fisheries and Oceans, the Coast Guard continues to protect mariners in Canadian waters using modern navigation and safety systems supplemented by 264 major lightstations and approximately 20,000 marine aids. Canadians have always taken great pride in their historical lighthouses, and the Coast Guard continues to work toward preserving these beautiful landmarks for future generations to admire.

COVE ISLAND LIGHTHOUSE

Geographical Position:
Latitude 45°19'37" N
Longitude 81°44'07" W
Georgian Bay, Lake Huron, Ontario
Building period: 1855-1859
Architect/Builder: John Brown
Construction Material: Stone
Tower Height: 36 meters
Focal Plane Height: 30.8 meters

Equipment: To the best of our knowledge the tower still has the original second-order dioptric lens whose lighting apparatus has progressed over the years from Argand lamps with whale oil, to flat wick-lamp for colza and coal oil, to coal oil vapor, to its present form of a light bulb.

General: The opening of the Bruce Peninsula for settlement in the mid-1850s, a free-trade agreement with the United States in 1854, and the building of the Sault Ste. Marie Canal in 1855 prompted the Government of Upper Canada to embark on an ambitious plan to build a network of lighthouses along the Great Lakes in the 1850s. The most impressive and well-preserved of these towers is Cove Island Lighthouse. It took four years to quarry stone and build the tower. Between 1855 and 1859 the tower took shape on an island in one of Canada's most scenic areas, the heart of the Great Lakes. In the 19th and early 20th centuries the tower allowed traders to bring goods from Northern Ontario to Southern Ontario's industrial plants and canals. Today the tower is a favorite landmark of thousands of recreational boaters every summer. Cove Island is also part of the Fathom Five National Marine Park in Lake Huron.

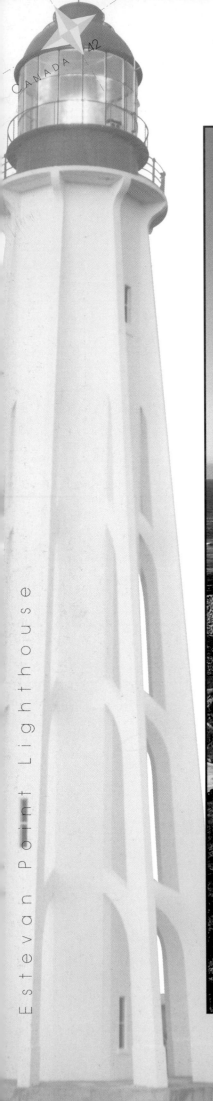

ESTEVAN POINT LIGHTHOUSE

Geographical Position:
Latitude 49°23'00" N
Longitude 126°32'32" W
West Coast of Vancouver Island
Building year: 1909
Architect/Builder:
Col. William P. Anderson
Construction Material: Reinforced concrete
Tower Height: 30.5 meters
Focal Plane Height: 38.1 meters

General: Estevan Point Lighthouse was the first light seen by early 20th century mariners sailing across the Pacific Ocean as they approached Canada. Colonel William P. Anderson, Chief Engineer of the Department of Marine and Fisheries, was the ambitious and innovative designer and overseer of the construction of the Estevan Point Tower. His influence in the federal civil service and an increase in federal government revenues were the prime motivators for the construction of a distinct tower on Estevan Point in 1909. Anderson used the opportunity presented by Canada's need for another major lighthouse on its Pacific coast to pioneer the use of reinforced concrete and flying buttresses in lighthouse construction. Steel rods meshed with poured concrete provided Canada with a stable and inexpensive tower. Buttresses of reinforced concrete, added by Anderson to further stabilize the tower, make the 30-meter-tall tower seem taller and gives it a rocket ship appearance. The lighthouse on Estevan Point became well known during the Second World War, as the area surrounding the tower was allegedly shelled by a Japanese submarine in 1942, without damaging the massive lighthouse.

ILE VERTE LIGHTHOUSE

Geographical Position:
Latitude 48°03'04" N
Longitude 69°25'29" W
St. Lawrence River
Building period: 1806-1809
Architect/Builder: Edward Cannon
Construction Material: Stone
Focal Plane Height: 16.5 meters

General: In 1809, after four years of construction, Ile Verte became the first lighthouse to grace the shores of the St. Lawrence River. The massive circular stone tower served as a model for lighthouses built along the seaway. Making this essential waterway's rapids safe was a high priority for the Québec government. It facilitated the development of the province and much of Canada by allowing marine traffic to travel deep into the industrial heart of the country. Ile Verte's construction is considered a milestone in the development of a system of safe waterways in Canada. Its guiding light helped solidify the reputation of Montreal and further inland ports as safe and prosperous trading centers in the 19th century. The longevity of the Ile Verte tower — a regional summer tourist attraction and a federal historical monument as the second oldest operational lighthouse in Canada — can be attributed to its solid design, building and strategic siting.

Equipment: The lantern has been modified several times in keeping with evolving technology and was automated in 1969. The current lantern is a DCB-10 supplied by Hydro-Québec. A new lantern was to be installed at the site sometime in 1998.

POINT AMOUR LIGHTHOUSE

Geographical Position:
Latitude 51°27'26" N
Longitude 56°51'35" W
Forteau Bay, Labrador
Building period: 1854-1857
Architect/Builder: Charles
François-Xavier Baby
Construction Material: Limestone
Tower Height: 36 meters

General: Point Amour Lighthouse, built on a barren and windswept point, helped tame the northern entrance to the Straits of Belle Isle. It was lit in 1858 after three years of construction. The tower is one of four "Imperial Towers" — so named because Great Britain funded their construction. These exceptionally tall lighthouses were built along the St. Lawrence Seaway in the 1850s to support Canada's booming intercontinental marine trade and the growing steamship industry. Quicker and less weather-dependent steamships were becoming the preferred cargo ships; however, they were expensive to run and their owners wanted to use the most direct routes to international ports. The tower on Point Amour allowed mariners to safely navigate a previously dangerous section of

the most direct trading route between central Canada's ports and Europe. Constructed with massive quantities of limestone and sheathed in cedar shingles, Point Amour is the second tallest lighthouse in Canada and has been recognized as a provincial historic site.

Equipment: The lantern has been modified several times in keeping with evolving technology and was automated in 1969. The current lantern is a DCB-10 supplied by Hydro-Québec. A new lantern was to be installed at the site sometime in 1998.

SAMBRO ISLAND LIGHTHOUSE

Geographical Position:
Latitude 44°26'12" N
Longitude 63°33'48" W
Building period: 1758-1759
Construction Material: Stone
Tower Height: 25 meters
Focal Plane Height: 42.7 meters

General: On October 2, 1758, the General Assembly of Nova Scotia passed an act and appropriated 1,000 British pounds from the duties paid by colonists on liquors. This money was used to help build what would become the oldest operational lighthouse in North America, on Sambro Island. A year later, the 60-foot-tall octagonal tower was erected atop the island of granite and lit. The tower was later raised to a height of 79 feet.

For almost 250 years, the red and white striped tower has been warding off mariners from the island's rocky shoals and guiding them safely into Halifax Harbor, Nova Scotia. This beacon has helped guide historic mariners such as the famous explorer and discoverer of Hawaii, Captain James Cook. General James Wolfe also used the lighthouse to guide him through Halifax Harbor on his way to conquering New France. Sambro Island's lighthouse was also the last sight of North America for thousands of Allied sailors as they sailed to fight in the First and Second World Wars.

Equipement

In 1834, Sambro's original lantern was described as having 8 large wooden posts, nearly a foot square, as uprights. The lantern's 128 small glass panes were held together by a combination of these uprights and some wooden sashes. During the same year a fog cannon was sent to Sambro. The firing of the cannon warned

ships away from the harbor's rocky shores. Thirty years later an improved lantern with plate glass and reflectors was imported from Great Britain. In 1906 an octagonal concrete wall was added to the octagonal stone walls of the tower and surmounted by a first-order circular iron lantern. This lantern was taken down from the tower in 1968. An aluminum lantern housing a DCB36 airport beacon was installed shortly afterward.

Chile

Chilean Maritime Signalling Service

Chile has a surface of 756,945 km² whose main characteristic is a vast coastline 4,270 km long where 5,900 islands are found. Its geographical configuration is very diverse, consisting of channels, fjords, and dangers to navigation. Since the beginning of the Republic Chile saw the need to install aids to navigation, particularly lighthouses. Some of these lighthouses have become famous and known by mariners all over the world.

Archipelagoes extend along the southern Chilean coast from Chiloé Island to Cape Horn, the southernmost point of the South American continent. In these islands are concentrated the most important Chilean lighthouses, some of which are some 100 years old. The builder of these lighthouses was George Slight.

Initial oversight of these lighthouses fell to the Lighthouse Office, founded on May 20, 1867, under the Secretariat of the Navy. Since that time the duties and responsibilities of lighthouse management have been transferred to the National Marine Signaling Service under the General Directorate of Maritime Territory and Merchant Marine. The National Marine Signaling Service consists of the Maritime Signaling Service (main offices) and 5 signaling depots located in Iquique, Valparaíso, Talcahuano, Puerto Montt, and Punta Arenas. The objective of this service is to establish, maintain, repair, and operate an effective system of coastal and river aids to navigation in the national territory.

ISLOTE EVANGELISTAS LIGHTHOUSE

Geographical Position:
Latitude 52°24' S
Longitude 75°06' W
Magellan Strait — Pacific Ocean
Commissioned: September 1896
Architect/Builder: George Slight,
Scottish engineer
Construction Material: Stone and
cement tower; concrete-covered metal
structure houses.
Tower Height: 11 meters
Focal Plane Height: 58 meters

General: The construction of this lighthouse deserves a special mention for the extraordinary effort it took build. The obstacle in this instance stemmed from the location of this isolated rock, which is near the western mouth of the Magellan Straight, 18 miles from the nearest archipelago and 240 miles from the nearest inhabited place. It is considered one of the most difficult to supply in all Latin America and one of the most isolated in the world.

Description: The house is in the English style with stone walls 1 meter thick, lined inwardly with wooden partitions. It consists of a cylindrical concrete tower at the lower section and metal at the upper section, joined to the house and painted white with horizontal red band. It also has a metallic cage of 3.6 meters in diameter, a 500 mm lantern with acrylic optic and a beam intensity of 541,000 candelas for the white light. The energy is provided by 2 generators which each work for 12 hours. Rain supplies the water.

BAHIA FELIX LIGHTHOUSE

Geographical Position:
Latitude 52°58' S
Longitude 74°04' W
Magellan Strait — Pacific Ocean
Commissioned: May 1907
Architect/Builder: Started by Luis
Camuzi and finished by George Slight
Construction Material: Granite
Tower Height: 14.2 meters
Focal Plane Height: 30 meters

General: Built because a light was required by navigators entering the Magellan Strait from the west, either using the sea route after seeing the Islote Evangelistas lighthouse, or taking the inside passage.

Description: Lighthouse with accommodations, built in granite and consisting of 10 rooms. It also houses a Customs Office, a carpentry room, and an engine room. It

has a jetty and a heliport which are joined by rail. Iron tower, half with wood cladding, painted white with horizontal red bands. Rotating lighting system, 60 watt lamps, CC-8 and a luminous intensity of 42,000 candelas. White light.

ISLA MAGDALENA LIGHTHOUSE

Geographical Position:
Latitude 52°55' S
Longitude 70°34' W
Magellan Strait — Pacific Ocean
Commissioned: April 1902
Architect/Builder: George Slight,
Scottish engineer / Causa and Chiartano
Construction Material: Bricks and
concrete
Tower Height: 13.5 meters
Focal Plane Height: 49 meters

General: This lighthouse was built almost 100 years ago to mark one of the most important routes that joins the Atlantic Ocean with the Pacific Ocean, through the Magellan Strait. It was an important commercial route when the Panama Canal did not exist and ships had to use the longer and more dangerous southern route. Situated in Isla Magdalena, already famous for its colonies of penguins, it was declared a Historical National Monument in 1976.

Description: Automatic lighthouse consisting of a house-lighthouse of English style with solid construction of 318 square meters, stone foundations, and concrete walls. It has 10 rooms which were inhabited by keepers until the mid 1950s. Cylindrical concrete tower joined to the house, painted white with horizontal red stripe. It has a 250 mm clear Fresnel lens with standard CC-8, 36 watt lamps and a luminous intensity of 35,000 candelas.

CABO RAPER LIGHTHOUSE

Geographical Position:
Latitude 46°49' S
Longitude 75°37' W
Golfo de Penas — Pacific Ocean
Commissioned: November 1914
Architect/Builder: George Slight, Scottish engineer
Construction Material: Reinforced concrete
Tower Height: 14 meters
Focal Plane Height: 61 meters

General: Lighthouse marks the sailing route through Golfo de Penas toward the inner channels in the southern zone. Navigation here is very difficult due to the bad conditions of the sea, with waves an average of 6 meters high.

Description: Lighthouse with accommodations in a place of very difficult access. It is located 8,000 meters from the pier, where there is a refuge consisting of 2 rooms. House of reinforced concrete in English style, with interior wooden lining joined to the tower, consisting of 15 rooms, 4 of them being bedrooms. Lower concrete tower with cast iron upper part and access through interior of the house. Painted white with horizontal red band. 500 mm rotating lantern, 60 watt lamp and 38,000 candelas.

PUNTA DUNGENESS LIGHTHOUSE

Geographical Position:
Latitude 52°24' S
Longitude 68°26' W
Entrance of Magellan Strait — Pacific Ocean
Commissioned: February 1899
Architect/Builder: Alan Brebner, engineer
Construction Material: Iron tower, house of concrete
Tower Height: 25 meters
Focal Plane Height: 32 meters

General: This lighthouse marks the eastern entry of the Magellan Strait, coming from the Atlantic Ocean. It has historical importance, since it is an important landmark in the dispute about sovereignty on the Magellan Strait, a coveted commercial route.

Description: Lighthouse with accommodations, located next to the border between Chile and Argentina. House of solid construction, English style consisting of 9 rooms. Iron tower joined to the house, painted white with red bands. Rotational illumination system with metal halide lamps, 440 watt, 220 volt, 42,000 candelas. It also has an engine room 20 meters from the principal house.

Cuba

Lighthouse Service of the Republic of Cuba

In Cuba all the responsibility for the establishment, control, performance, and development of the National System of Aids to Navigation is under the Hydrographic and Geodesic Service of the Republic of Cuba (HGS), which is composed of the Hydrographic and Geodesic Direction (HGD) and the Entrepreneurial Group GEOCUBA. Both entities coordinate their efforts for the purpose of preserving the safety of navigation, human life at sea and the marine environment, the coastline and atmosphere from pollution, in accordance with national and international regulations. The governmental functions of inspection, management, international representation and funding related to aids to navigation belong to the HGD. Those functions related to the production and services are a responsibility of the Entrepreneurial Group GEOCUBA.

The HGS of the Republic of Cuba operates 1,070 aids to navigation: 794 of them are lit, 5 are racons, 16 are manned lighthouses and 62 are automatic lighthouses, 551 are beacons and 435 are buoys.

The HGS is now carrying out a program to improve the aids to navigation system, which includes the implementation of Differential GPS, the use of remote control and monitoring systems, the automation of the manned lighthouses and the evaluation of the quantity and quality of aids needed to provide the most reliable, efficient and economical service.

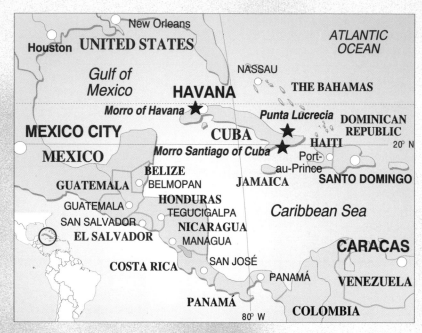

PUNTA LUCRECIA LIGHTHOUSE

Geographical Position:
Latitude 21°04'15" N
Longitude 75°37'13" W
Date of building: 1868
Architect/Builder:
Restituto Blancafort
Construction Material:
Square hewn stone

History: On February 12, 1858, the government's Political Secretary approached the Public Building Inspector about a projected lighthouse for a place called Punta Lucrecia.

The first design was made by Commandant of Engineers Saturnino Ruedas, but the third design by Restituto Blancafort was finally chosen.

Due to financial difficulties construction was stopped on December 21, 1862, by the Civil Superior Government; however, work was finally completed in May 1868. The light was ready for service on October 10, 1868, the same day Carlos Manuel de Céspedes, now known as the Father of the Nations, freed his slaves and asked them to fight for Cuba against Spain.

On December 21 of 1868 a few Mambises attacked the lighthouse and destroyed the optical apparatus. The light was relit on May 10, 1870.

LIGHTHOUSE MORRO OF HAVANA

Geographical Position:
Latitude 23°08'59" N
Longitude 82°21'263" W
Date of building: First tower, before 1563;
Present tower, 1844
Construction Material: Square hewn
stone

History: In 1610 when the Castle of the Three Kings of Morro was built by the architect Batiste Antonelli, the lighthouse was incorporated into the new building. It was destroyed in 1762 during the British takeover of Havana, but was rebuilt by the Spanish a year later. The light was originally powered by burning wood.

At 7:30 A.M. on July 24, 1845, the Fresnel optical apparatus came into use. Its production had been supervised by Augustin Fresnel himself, who referred to it as one of the most perfect optics ever made. It was displayed at the Paris Public Fair that year. As part of Morro Cabañas Park and the historical center of the old township of San Cristobal of Havana, the area was designated as a World Heritage Site by UNESCO in 1982.

The most important facet of the lighthouse was that it witnessed in succession the transfer of the sovereignty of Cuba to Spain, Britain, and the United States of America, and finally the liberation of the island by the Cuban people. Now the lighthouse is a very popular tourist attraction.

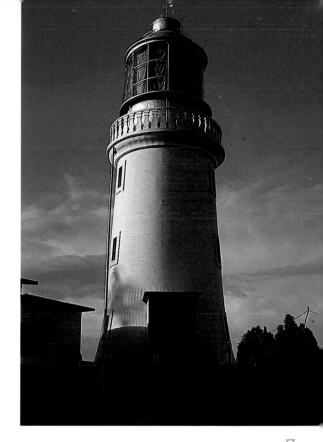

LIGHTHOUSE MORRO SANTIAGO OF CUBA

Geographical Position:
Latitude 19°58'1" N
Longitude 75°52'7" W
Building date: 1842
Construction Material: Square hewn
stone

History: The second lighthouse of Cuba owes its construction to the increase of navigation and trade with the Santiago of Cuba.

It began as a project by the Belgian Consul Luis Antonio Werbrugge and the merchants of the city who promised to help finance the building in 1840. Work was finished in April 1842. Its lantern, modeled on an existing lantern in a British port, was imported from New York. The lighthouse had an iron tower that was octagonal in form.

During the Hispanic American War the tower and the lighting apparatus, part of the fortress of Morro, were destroyed. They were reconstructed in 1899 with the help of the American Lighthouse Service, who supplied the lighting equipment.

The construction of a new 12 meter truncated stone tower began in 1914. The optical apparatus, lantern, and other items were bought from the French firm Barbier Bénard and Turenne in the following year, but because the First World War was then in progress, it was impossible to receive them until 1923. The lighthouse did not enter service until 1923.

The light was electrified in 1953, and the lighthouse is now a tourist attraction as part of the historic fortress of Morro Santiago of Cuba.

United States of America

The United States Coast Guard

The United States Coast Guard is the nation's oldest continuous seagoing service, tracing its history back to 1790. It is the amalgamation of five maritime agencies: the Revenue Cutter Service, the Lifesaving Service, the U.S. Lighthouse Service, the Steamboat Inspection Service and the Bureau of Navigation. Through its antecedents, the United States Coast Guard is one of the oldest organizations under the Federal Government. In times of peace it operates in the Department of Transportation, serving as the country's premier agency for promoting marine safety and enforcing federal maritime laws. The United States Coast Guard is active in twelve mission areas. They include Search and Rescue, Aids to Navigation, Waterways Management, Boating Safety, Environmental Response, Ice Operations, Marine Science, Maritime Law Enforcement, Marine Inspection, Marine Licensing, Port Security and Safety, and Defense Operations. In times of war, or on the direction of the President, it is attached to the Navy Department and carries out various missions for national security.

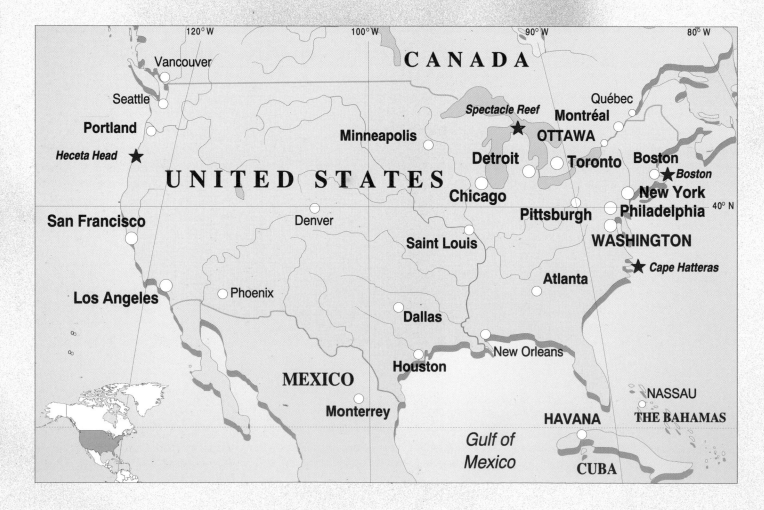

BOSTON LIGHTHOUSE

Geographical Position:
Latitude 42°19'7" N
Longitude 70°19'7" W
Little Brewster Island, Boston Harbor
Date of building:
First lighthouse, 1716
Present lighthouse, 1789
Architect: William Payne and Captain Zechariah Tuthill
Construction Material: Foundation made of granite ledge. Structure made of rubble stone with brick lining
Tower Height: 29.87 meters
Focal Plane Height: 31.10 meters

General:

This site is the first lighthouse built in what became the United States. In the early 18th century, merchants became concerned that vessels carrying their goods have safe entry into the port. A committee appointed by the legislature quickly recognized the merchants' fears and saw the necessity for a navigational aid in the harbor. On September 14, 1716, the keeper displayed the light for the first time. The light station consisted of a tall masonry tower, a two-story dwelling and several small sheds. The light in the lantern was supplied by either candles or lamps. To pay for the operation of the light, the court levied tonnage dues on cargo going into and out of the harbor. In 1719 the court placed a cannon on the island to serve as a fog signal, the country's first.

At the beginning of the American Revolution, to prevent the signal from assisting British vessels, American troops removed the lamps from the lighthouse's lantern and set fire to the structure. British attempts to repair the tower were rebuffed by American forces. As they evacuated Boston, the British blew up the tower.

At the end of the war, the Massachusetts legislature appropriated funds to rebuild the lighthouse on the island. There is no evidence that any materials from the old lighthouse were used in the new 27.1 meter white conical stone tower with a second-order lens whose light is 31.1 meters above sea level. Today, Boston Harbor Light is the only remaining American lighthouse to be staffed by Coast Guard personnel. (Extract from *Great American Lighthouses* by F. Ross Holland, Jr.)

UNITED STATES

CAPE HATTERAS LIGHTHOUSE

Geographical Position:
Latitude 35°15'03" N
Longitude 75°31'02" W
Outer banks of North Carolina
Date of building:
First lighthouse, 1797
Second lighthouse, 1870
Architect: Dexter Stetson
Material: Foundation made of granite and timber. Structure made of brick, cast iron, and stone
Tower Height: 63.40 meters
Focal Plane Height: 58.20 meters

General:
Located on the Outer Banks, in the middle of the stretch of coast that came to be known as the Graveyard of the Atlantic, this lighthouse was regarded in the 19th century as the most important light on the East Coast. Its principal purpose has been to warn coastal traffic about the dangerous and shallow Diamond Shoals, which extend for more than 8 miles from the cape. In 1851 the committee investigating the condition of the country's lighthouse system recommended that this lighthouse be the first one fitted with a first-order Fresnel lens and that, for the light to be seen better at a distance, the tower be raised to 150 feet. Two years later the new Lighthouse Board implemented both recommendations, raising the focal plane to 140 feet. With the onset of the Civil War, the Confederate soldiers put the Cape Hatteras lighthouse out of operation by removing the lens, but by June 1862, the Union forces had it back in service.

At the end of the war the Lighthouse Board noted that the tower was beyond repair and urged that a new tower be built. Fearing the old tower would topple over, charges were set off in it to bring it down.

The new conical brick tower was 193 feet tall. It was and still is the tallest lighthouse tower in America. The focal plane of its first-order lens is 191 feet above sea level. To make the tower a better daymark, the Lighthouse Board had it painted with black-and-white spiral bands in 1873. Erosion has been a threat to the new tower through the years. Although many techniques were tried, no preventive measures have been effective. In 1936 the Bureau of Lighthouses built a skeleton tower a mile from the 1870 light and moved the light to that point. At the same time the bureau gave the tower to the National Park soldiers Service.

Erosion once again threatens the light tower. It is likely that the lighthouse, now a beloved landmark, will be moved. Meanwhile, the light station is still open to the public, although the tower, in need of repairs, is now closed. (Extract from *Great American Lighthouses* by F. Ross Holland, Jr.)

Cape Hatteras lighthouse

HECETA HEAD LIGHTHOUSE

Geographical Position:
Latitude 44°08'02" N
Longitude 124°07'07" W
North of Siuslaw River in Oregon
Date of building: 1894
Material: Brick and stucco
Tower Height: 17.1 meters
Focal Plane Height: 62.5 meters

Description: Lighted on March 30, 1894, this 56-foot conical masonry tower was erected to guide ships along the section of coast north of the Siuslaw River. Its first-order Fresnel lens, whose focal plane is 205 feet above sea level, lighted a dark area between Yaquina Head and Cape Arago, a distance of some 90 miles. The light is automated. But a number of buildings survive, including the oil house near the tower and one of the old dwellings that is now on Forest Service land. The picturesque setting of the lighthouse on this rugged, rocky coast has made the old structure a popular subject for photographers. The grounds of the old light station are open to the public; however, the lighthouse is not open. The dwelling, restored by the Siuslaw National Forest, is leased to Lane Community College. (Extract from *Great American Lighthouses* by F. Ross Holland, Jr.)

Spectacle Reef lighthouse

SPECTACLE REEF LIGHTHOUSE

Geographical Position:
Latitude 45°46'04" N
Longitude 84°08'02" W
Lake Huron, eastern end of Straits
of Mackinac
Date of building: 1870–1874
Architect: Major O. M. Poe
Material: Limestone
Tower Height: 28.3 meters
Focal Plane Height: 26.20 meters

General: After two large schooners went down in the waters of the Straits of Mackinac near Spectacle Reef in the fall of 1867, Congress appropriated $100,000 to begin construction of a lighthouse. A total of $406,000 was spent to complete the project, by far the most expensive lighthouse built on the Great Lakes up to that time. When finished, it stood 86 feet high, the tallest and most impressive example of monolithic stone lighthouse construction on the Lakes. The need for an underwater foundation, the difficult climate of northern Lake Huron, and the isolated site combined to make this project a major engineering feat. Scammon's Harbor at Les Cheneaux, some 16 miles from the reef, served as a base for materials and supplies. Over a 4-year period, a workforce of more than 200 men, using two lighthouse tenders and a dozen other vessels, struggled during the shipping season to erect the lighthouse and displayed the permanent light for the first time on June 1, 1874. This light station was automated in the early 1970s. (Extract from *The Northern Lights Lighthouses of the Upper Great Lakes* by Charles K. Hyde.)

MAKAPUU POINT LIGHTHOUSE

Geographical Position:
Latitude 21°18'06" N
Longitude 157°38'09" W
Oahu island, Hawaii
Date of building: 1909
Architect: Lieutenant Colonel F. M. Casey
Material: Masonry and concrete
Tower Height: 14.0 meters
Focal Plane Height: 128.0 meters

Description: In its 1905 report the Lighthouse Board noted that "all deep-sea commerce between Honolulu and Puget Sound, the Pacific Coast of the United States, Mexico and Central America, including Panama, passes Makapuu Head, and . . . there is not a single light on the whole northern coast of the Hawaiian Islands to guide ships or warn them of the approach to land, after a voyage of several thousands miles." The board selected a site nearly 400 feet above sea level to construct the white cylindrical 46-foot concrete tower on. The hyper-radiant lens assigned to it is the largest U.S. lens in use, with an inside diameter of 8.5 feet. The focal plane of its light is 420 feet above sea level, making it visible for 28 miles. The station received a radio beacon in 1927. Still active, the light of its old hyper-radiant lens is now automated. The site is accessible, but the light at present is not open to the public. (Extract from *Great American Lighthouses* by F. Ross Holland, Jr.)

Jamaica

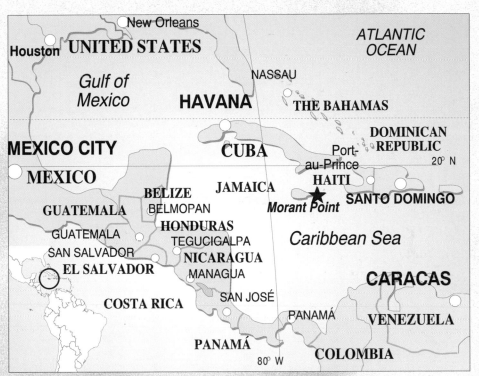

MORANT POINT LIGHTHOUSE

Geographical Position:
Latitude 17°55' N
Longitude 76°12' W
Building year: 1842
Architect/Builder: Axel Gordon, civil engineer, London
Construction material: Cast iron
Tower Height: 24.4 meters

Description: At the extreme east end of Jamaica, this lighthouse carries a revolving white light, elevated 115 feet above high water, and is visible at a distance of 21 miles at sea in clear weather. The illuminant is petroleum vapor used with an incandescent mantle giving an apparent intensity of approximately 19,000 candelas. The lens consists of 8 symmetrical panels with dioptric and upper catadioptric portions revolving once every 8 minutes, thus providing a single white flash every minute.

Peru

LA MARINA LIGHTHOUSE

Geographical Position:
Latitude 12°07'12" S
Longitude 77°02'18" W
Building year: 1917
Architect/Builder: Chance Brothers
Construction Material: Cast iron, then concrete
Tower Height: 22 meters

History: The present lighthouse, located in Lima, is considered part of Peru's maritime heritage. This lighthouse was re-established in a park called La Plaza del Navigante in September 1973. The park, located in the middle of the Miraflores district, was inaugurated on December 1 of the same year. The lighthouse's history dates back to January 4, 1917, when Law No. 2417 authorized its construction at Punta Coles on the southern coast of Peru. Chance Brothers built the lighthouse according to the design of the famous architect, Gustave Eiffel. Its fourth-order light was lit on February 24, 1920.

Kerosene was the original energy source for the lighthouse. In 1938, a gas AGA optic was installed. Today, the lighthouse uses a PR50 optic which has been modified to allow for electric power. The light has a range of 22 nautical miles.

In 1974, following the re-establishment of the lighthouse, a concrete replacement was built at Punta Coles. This lighthouse kept the original shape and technical characteristics.

TORRE RELOJ LIGHTHOUSE

Geographical Position:
Latitude 12°3'17" S
Longitude 77°8'40" W
Building year: 1889
Architect/Builder: Latin America Corporation SA
Main construction material: Steel
Tower Height: 12 meters
Focal Plane Height: 15 meters

History: The first lighthouses and direction lights were installed in various places of the Peruvian coastline between 1887 and 1890. It is during this period that the Torre Reloj del Muelle de Guerra (the watch tower of the war pier) was built in Calloa harbor. Torre Reloj was one of the first lighthouses to use a steel structure rather than wood.

In 1889 an English team built the lighthouse and the pier. They called it Torre Reloj because an analog watch, manufactured by Smith & Sons, stands at the top part of the structure.

This lighthouse remains engraved in the memory of many generations of mariners and others who have called at Calloa, the first Peruvian port.

In July 1890 it witnessed the departure and return of the soldiers who took part in the South Pacific War battles.

Today the lighthouse remains an aid to navigation, showing its original characteristics. Its light has a range of 3.3 miles.

Uruguay

History

Lighthouses originally belonged to private owners, later to the Ministerio de Obras Publicas, and since 1933 to the Navy Administration. The Servicio de Iluminación y Balizamiento (SERBA) is the Navy Service that maintains the buoyage system. This system includes the lighthouses distributed along the coast.

The lighthouses are the original structures, most of which still use the original light equipment, with a mechanical weight system for the rotation of the light.

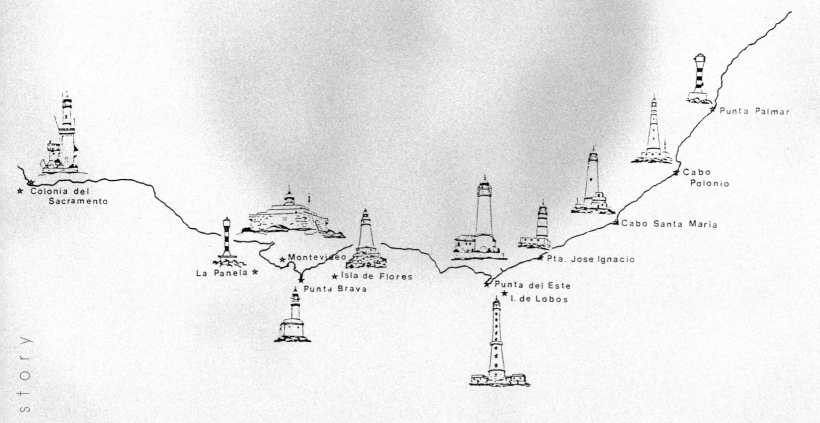

PUNTA DEL ESTE LIGHTHOUSE

Geographical Position:
Latitude 34°58'08" S
Longitude 54°57'05" W
Rio de la Plata external border
Commissioned: March 1, 1860
Architect/Builder: Juan Tomas Libarona
Construction Material: Masonry
Tower Height: 35 meters
Focal Plane Height: 44 meters

General: The lighthouse has a circular white tower, a dome with red and white radial bands and a white building at the base.

The lighting system is an L. Sautter Lemonier & Cie second-order optic, powered by electricity. The prism has dioptric and catadioptric lenses (13 central dioptrics, 12 upper catadioptrics and 5 lower catadioptrics).

It produces 1 white flash of 152,530 candelas every 8 seconds with a luminous nominal range of 20.8 nautical miles.

Historic description: The original lighthouse for Isla de Lobos was built by Juan Tomas de Libarona. In 1858 the Ministerio considered moving the lighthouse to Punta del Este because the light frightened seals. The lighthouse was incorporated into the navigation service in 1860.

In 1923 the lighthouse was reconstructed and new service buildings were built.

CABO SANTA MARIA LIGHTHOUSE

Geographical Position:
Latitude 34°40'04" S
Longitude 54°09'06" W
Santa Maria Cape, Atlantic Coast
Commissioned: May 10, 1874
Architect/Builder: Engineer Cerruti
Construction Material: Masonry and stone
Tower Height: 30 meters
Focal Plane Height: 42 meters

General: The lighthouse has a circular white tower with white buildings at the base. The dome has red and white radial bands.

The lighting system is electric. It is an L. Sautter Lemonier & Cie first-order rotating optic, with bronze wheels on a steel track.

The prism has dioptric and catadioptric lenses (7 central dioptrics, 11 upper catadioptrics and 4 lower catadioptrics). It produces 1 white flash of 117,267 candelas every 60 seconds. The national electricity network provides energy for the lamp and rotative motor.

Historic description: The construction of the lighthouse was troubled. In a severe storm, the tower was destroyed by lightning, killing 15 workers.

Two years later, the Empresa de Faros del Rio de la Plata company lit the lantern that is used today.

CERRO DE MONTEVIDEO LIGHTHOUSE

Geographical Position:
Latitude 34°53'18" S
Longitude 55°15'34" W
Rio de la Plata,
Fort General Artigas
Montevideo Peak, Montevideo City
Commissioned: 1802
Construction Material: Masonry
Tower Height: 8 meters
Focal Plane Height: 148 meters

General: The lighthouse has a circular tower, a dome, and buildings, all painted white. It is located in Fort General Artigas. The light system was designed by Henry Lepaute of Paris. The optic is third order, rotating on an electrically powered mercury plate. The prism has dioptric and catadioptric lenses (9 central dioptrics with 3 focus, 10 upper catadioptrics, and 4 lower catadioptrics). It produces 3 white flashes of 75,530 candelas every 10 seconds. The luminous nominal range is 18 nautical miles. The national electricity network supplies power to the lighthouse.

Historic description: The Montevideo Peak lighthouse was first constructed in the Rio de la Plata in 1802. Nine years later, it was moved to Fort Montevideo Peak (today, Fort General Artigas).
A fixed light of clay lamps burning colt grease lit the lamp from 1802 to 1818. The second light, designed by Priest Jose Arrieta, was a rotating system that used whale oil. In 1836 a new lighthouse was built because the former was destroyed by lightning. In 1852 the lighting system was changed to seven mineral oil lamps placed in the center and vertexes of a hexagon. In 1936 a kerosene system was installed. On December 6, 1942, the present lighting system was installed.

ISLA DE FLORES LIGHTHOUSE

Geographical Position:
Latitude 34°56'45" S
Longitude 55°55'56" W
Rio de la Plata, Flores Island
Commissioned: January 1, 1828
Architect/Builder: Ramon Artagabeitia
Construction Material: Masonry and stone
Tower Height: 19.5 meters
Focal Plane Height: 37 meters

General: The lighthouse has a truncated conical stone tower with external and internal masonry painted white, a dome painted with red and white radial bands, and white buildings at the base.
The AGA PR-50 light is from Stockholm, Sweden. The optic is third order. The prism has dioptric and catadioptric lenses (11 upper catadioptrics and 6 lower catadioptrics). An electric generator powers the lamp and the rotation motor. The optic produces 2 white flashes of 63,687 candelas every 16 seconds. The luminous nominal range is 18.6 nautical miles.

Historic description: The first signal light in Flores Island was provided by the warship Nuestre Señora de Loreto, placed on the most suitable point on the island. It operated until 1798. After a long period of various owners, General Lecor transferred the light to Dr. Obes during the period of Lusitanian rule over the Eastern Province. In 1818, with the buildings under construction, a storm destroyed the ships carrying workers and materials to the island, and the governor left the buildings unfinished. Construction on the lighthouse began again in 1825. On July 4, 1826 the works were transferred to Ramon Artagabeitia. The lighthouse, a typical early 19th century Lusitanian building, was incorporated into the navigation service on January 1, 1828 and construction was completed later that year.

COLONIA DEL SACRAMENTO LIGHTHOUSE

Geographical Position:
Latitude 34°28'22" S
Longitude 57°61'06" W
Rio de la Plata
Colonia del Sacramento City
Commissioned: January 24, 1855
Architect/Builder: Sociedad Porvenir de la Colonia
Construction Material: Masonry and stone
Tower Height: 26.92 meters
Focal Plane Height: 34 meters

General: The lighthouse has a circular tower painted white, a dome with white and red radial bands and a crumbling old building at its base.

The light system is an AGA LTBA-500, fourth order optic with L-500 lens, lit by acetylene gas. The prism has dioptric and catadioptric lenses (1 central dioptric, 5 lower catadioptrics and 5 upper cata-dioptrics). An electric generator powers the lamp and the rotation motor. It produces 1 red flash of 192 candelas every 9 seconds. The luminous nominal range is 6.4 nautical miles.

Historic description: The Colonia del Sacramento lighthouse was paid for with tariffs collected from ships visiting Uruguayan ports. Its construction was completed by a service concession to the Sociedad Porvenir de la Colonia on January 24, 1855.
It was incorporated into the navigation service in 1857.
The lighthouse is located in an old neighborhood of Colonia del Sacramento City. This neighborhood was declared a World Cultural Heritage site by UNESCO on December 5, 1995.

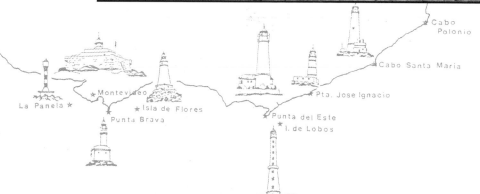

A S

I A

China

History

中国沿海五座历史文物灯塔分布示意图

China has a vast expanse of sea waters scattered all over with numerous islands and seaports. The coastline extends as long as 18,000 km. Aids to Navigation in China have a long history. An embryonic form of ATN appeared as early as the seventh century. With the development of maritime transport, the ATN were constantly improved and developed. The degree of automation and effectiveness of the equipment were gradually enhanced. To date, under the jurisdiction of the Maritime Safety Administration of the Ministry of Communications, a total of 2,601 aids comprising a mix of visual, audio and radio aids are operated. They not only serve to provide safe navigation for domestic and foreign vessels, but they also facilitate the development of trade between China and other countries, helping promote the growth of the national economy.

中国

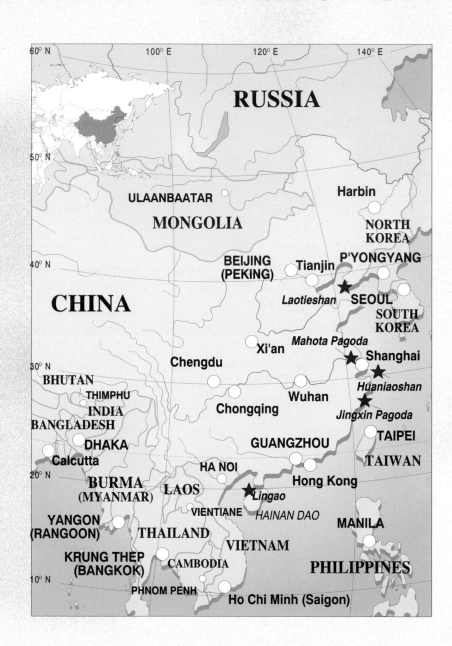

MAHOTA PAGODA LIGHTHOUSE

Geographical Position:
Latitude 31°03'12" N
Longitude 121°04'18" E
East China Sea, inner waters
of Shanghai Harbor
Commissioned: 874
Architect/Builder: Monk RuHai
Construction Material: Bricks and wood

General: Shanghai is the hub of water transportation in East China. In AD 874, Monk RuHai built the Mahota Pagoda in the middle of the Mao River, hanging a lantern from the top of the pagoda at night. Vessels sailing in the wide Mao River regarded this pagoda as a lighthouse.

Shanghai is situated at the entrance of the Changjiang River. The average yearly river discharge is 30,200 cubic meters per second, and the silt brought down by the flow approximates 500,000 tons per year. This results in sedimentation and formation of banks and shoals in and outside the entrance. Use of the pagoda as an aid to navigation extended only to the end of the Song Dynasty (AD 1279).

This pagoda was declared a national historical relic in 1962.

灯塔

JINGXIN PAGODA LIGHTS

Geographical Position:
Latitude 28°01'49" N (East pagoda)
28°01'48" N (West pagoda)
Longitude 120°38'38" E (East pagoda)
120°38'24" E (West pagoda)
East China Sea, on river, Wenzhou Harbor
Commissioned: 869 (East pagoda), 969 (West pagoda)
Construction Material: Bricks and wood

General: Thousands of years ago, there were two purposes for building pagodas on China's coast: 1) to pray to Buddha to subdue sea monsters and bless seamen, and 2) to show remarkable objects for distinct visual aids.

According to the annals of Wenzhou County, in the initial stage, only one pagoda (the east pagoda) was built for guiding vessels. After 100 years, another pagoda was built westward of the same island. The west pagoda is higher than the east one. Lining up the two pagodas indicates the middle of the narrow channel. Navigators still use these two pagodas as leading marks.

Both pagodas were declared national historical relics in June 1981.

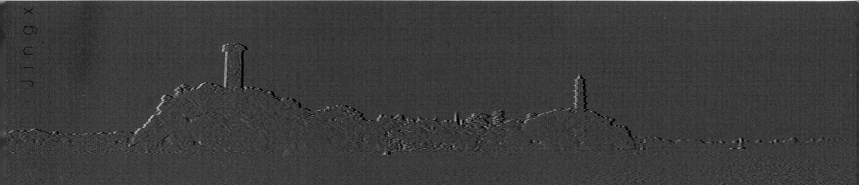

LINGAO LIGHTHOUSE (LAMKO IH)

Geographical Position:
Latitude 20°00'30" N
Longitude 109°42'15" E
South China Sea, Northwest cape
of Hainan Island
Commissioned: 1894
Architect/Builder: Chinese Maritime
Customs
Construction Material: Wrought iron

General: Lingao is the westernmost Chinese lighthouse. It is the first Chinese light seen by travelers arriving in China coastwise from Indochina, but travelers arriving via Hong Kong from the west must go out of their way to see it. Strategically situated at the northwest corner of Hainan Island, it commands the entrance to the Hainan Strait from the westward.

The apparatus is of fourth order and was established on November 15, 1894. Lingao remained with its original wick burner until 1930, when a vaporized petroleum burner with 35 mm incandescent mantle was installed. This change necessitated the conversion of the rotating machinery from the central spindle to the pedestal type. The improvement raised the power of the light from 10,000 to 110,000 candelas.

Description: In October 1994, new light equipment (parabolic reflector array PRB-46) was installed, which gives 1 white flash every 10 seconds with a range of 18 nautical miles in clear weather.

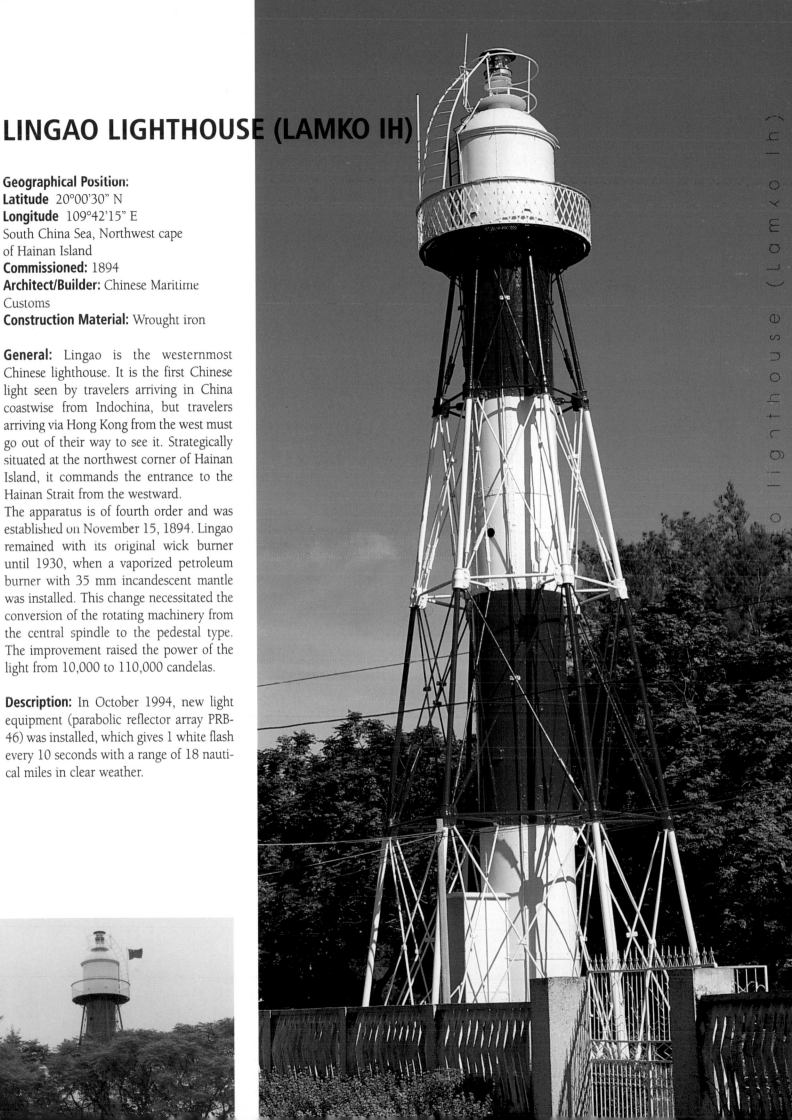

HUANIAOSHAN LIGHTHOUSE
(NORTH SADDLE LIGHTHOUSE)

Geographical Position:
Latitude 30°51'41" N
Longitude 122°40'17" E
East China Sea, entrance to Yangtze River and Shanghai Harbor
Commissioned: 1870
Architect/Builder: Chinese Maritime Customs
Construction Material: Round casting
Tower Height: 26 meters
Focal Plane Height: 31 meters

Huaniaoshan lighthouse

General: Huaniaoshan Lighthouse is the big light leading to the entrance to the Yangtze River and Shanghai Harbor. With its first-order light, electronic fog signal, and radio beacon, it may easily be considered the biggest station among the Chinese lights. It is situated on the northeast extremity of the island.

This lighthouse was established in 1870 by the Customs Marine Department of China. The tower is made of bricks with the lower-half painted white and the upper-half painted black. The original apparatus was a four-wick lamp burning vegetable oil at an intensity of 38,000 candelas and rotating with a period of one minute. At the end of 1916, a new first-order optical lens was installed, rotating on a mercury float. The lamp was also changed to an incandescent petroleum vapor burner having a single 110 mm mantle, creating 1 flash of 740,000 candelas every 15 seconds. The mantle was eventually changed to an electric Na-T1-In lamp (2,000 watts), raising the power to 1,600,000 candelas.

In 1923 a first-order diaphone fog signal was completed to take the place of the old fog guns. This signal was replaced in 1986 by Liec-300-5 long-range electric sound emitters.

In 1929 a wireless radio beacon was built and put into action here, a first in Chinese waters.

This lighthouse was declared a national historical relic in June 1988.

Description: First-order dioptric bull's-eyes lens (1840 mm diameter), radio beacon 500 watts and Liec-300-5 sound emitters.

LAOTIESHAN LIGHTHOUSE

Geographical Position:
Latitude 38°43'37" N
Longitude 121°08'03" E
Entrance of Bohai Sea
Commissioned: 1893
Architect/Builder: Chinese Maritime Customs
Construction Material: Round casting

General: This lighthouse on Laotieshan Promontory, about 12 km from Lushun Port, was one of the earliest aids to navigation instituted by Chinese Customs. Its purpose is to serve as a marking light for vessels approaching Lushun Port or Bohai Strait.

The first-order light was completed in 1893 and became the first apparatus rotating on a mercury float to be erected by the Customs lighthouse engineers. Early in 1895 it was passed to the Japanese for a few months, but was handed back in December of the same year. It was maintained by Customs until 1898, when it was taken over by the Russians. In April 1955, it was handed back to the Chinese People's Navy.

Laotieshan Lighthouse was placed under the jurisdiction of the Dalian Maritime Safety Administration of the Ministry of Communications in January 1983.

Description: Dioptric bull's-eye lens within an incandescent lamp (2,000 watts). Showing double white flashes every 30 seconds; 23 nautical mile range on main power supply.

A wireless radio beacon was built in 1959, located on a hill east of the lighthouse. The radio beacon was converted to a RBN/DGPS station in 1997.

Republic of Korea

PALMIDO LIGHTHOUSE

Geographical Position:
Latitude 37°21'18" N
Longitude 26°31'36" E
Yellow Sea
Commissioned: June 1903
Construction Material: Iron concrete
Tower Height: 7.9 meters
Focal Plane Height: 40 meters

General: This is the oldest constructed lighthouse in Korea. It was shut down during the Korean War, but the lighthouse keeper turned on the lamp to help landing operations in Inchon. The lighthouse is located at the mouth of Inchon Port.

Description: An 8-meter round iron concrete tower, painted white, supports a white lantern house with a sixth-order revolving optic. The optic produces 3 flashes of 800,000 candelas every 40 seconds. The focal height is 40 meters. Electricity is supplied by a diesel generator with a standby battery; equipped with a radio beacon and an air siren.

PUDO LIGHTHOUSE

Geographical Position:
Latitude 37°08'48" N
Longitude 126°21'00" E
Yellow Sea
Commissioned: April 1904
Construction Material: Stones
Tower Height: 12 meters
Focal Plane Height: 42 meters

General: This constructed lighthouse is located near Inchon Port.

Description: A 12-meter round stone tower, painted white, supports a white lantern house with an HY-610 mm revolving optic. The optic produces 1 flash of 40,000 candelas every 15 seconds and has a focal height of 42 meters. Electricity is supplied by the diesel generator with a standby battery; equipped with an electronic horn and racon.

ONGDO LIGHTHOUSE

Geographical Position:
Latitude 36°38'30" N
Longitude 126°00'36" E
Yellow Sea
Commissioned: April 1904
Construction Material:
Iron concrete
Tower Height: 14 meters
Focal Plane Height: 75 meters

General: This constructed lighthouse is located near Daisan Port.

Description: A 14-meter octagonal iron concrete tower, painted white, supports a white lantern house with a DCB-36 flashing optic. The optic produces 1 flash of 150,000 candelas every 15 seconds and has a focal height of 75 meters. Electricity is supplied by the diesel generator with a standby battery; equipped with an air siren.

CHANGGIGOT LIGHTHOUSE

Geographical Position:
Latitude 36°04'30" N
Longitude 129°34'18" E
East Sea of Korea
Commissioned: Décember 1903
Construction Material: Bricks
Tower Height: 26 meters
Focal Plane Height: 31 meters

General: It is the second-oldest constructed lighthouse in Korea. The lighthouse located at the mouth of Pohang Port and accommodates the lighthouse museum.
Description: A 26-meter octagonal brick tower, painted white, supports a white lantern house with a DCBR-24 projecting optic. The optic produces 1 flash of 300,000 candelas every 12 seconds and has a focal height of 31 meters. Electricity is supplied by the national electricity network with a standby diesel generator; equipped with a radio beacon and an air siren.

KOMUNDO LIGHTHOUSE

Geographical Position:
Latitude 34°01'12" N
Longitude 127°19'30" E
East Sea of Korea
Commissioned: April 1905
Construction Material: Bricks
Tower Height: 6.4 meters
Focal Plane Height: 69 meters

General: This constructed lighthouse is on the South Sea of the Korean Peninsula, used by mariners navigating the Cheju Strait.
Description: A 6-meter round brick tower, painted white, supports a white lantern house with a third-order revolving optic and 3 equally spaced catadioptric lens panels. The optic produces 1 flash of 100,000 candelas every 15 seconds and has a focal height of 69 meters. Electricity is supplied by the national electricity network with a standby diesel generator; equipped with a radio beacon and an air siren.

India

भारत

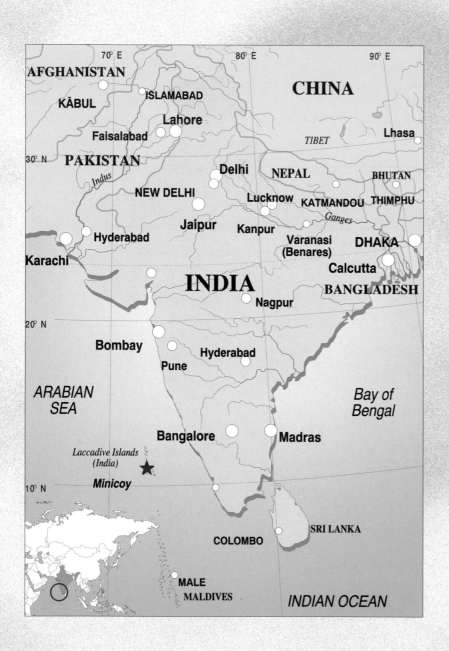

MINICOY LIGHTHOUSE

Geographical Position:
Latitude 08°16'0" N
Longitude 73°01'6" E
Arabian Sea
Building period: 1883 – 1885
Construction Material: Brick masonry, imported from Birmingham, England
Tower Height: 49.53 meters

History: Minicoy Island assumed great importance by virtue of its strategic location after the opening of the Suez Canal in 1869, which shortened the sea distance between Europe and the Far East by 4,000 miles. The British Government in consultation with Lord Rippon, then Governor General, decided in 1882 to construct a lighthouse on the island. As this island was full of coconut trees it was envisaged to construct a 49-meter high lighthouse tower to provide all-around visibility. The foundation stone was laid in 1883 and the ceremony of laying the first stone was performed by Howah Manika, the youngest daughter of the Amin of Minicoy, Mr. Bephanu.

Until 1934 the lighthouse was under direct control of the Board of Trade London. It was completely transferred along with lighthouses of Ceylon and Burma to a board

appointed by the Board of Trade London. Although India attained her independence on August 15, 1947, the British Government did not transfer administration of the lighthouse to India until April 1956. The de jure transfer of administration to the Government of India had to wait until September 19, 1963, as both houses of the British Parliament had to pass legislation which required the assent of the Queen of England.

It is reported that when the Union Jack was lowered and the Indian national tricolor was hoisted on the lighthouse on April 2, 1956, Mr. Rees, then Superintendent of Imperial Lighthouses who had specially come for the formal transfer of the lighthouses to the Government of India, could not utter a word, ran to his boat, and left the island.

Description: On February 2, 1885, the light was originally commissioned with a kerosene wick lamp enclosed in a lantern. In 1928 the wick lamp was replaced by a 35 mm petroleum vapor burner. In 1968 the burner was replaced with an 85 mm PV burner enclosed in a first-order optic. In 1995 the PV burner was replaced by a metal halide electric lamp.

Minicoy lighthouse

Japan

History

Entirely surrounded by sea, Japan is a country where maritime navigation has always been very active. Records show that for a long time, various systems had been used to guide the mariners: torchères, bonfires, and braziers maintained in stone lanterns.

By the middle of the 19th century, when Japan opened doors that had been kept closed to foreign people for more than two hundred years, it adopted for its lighthouses construction techniques used in France and in England. This is why most of these buidings, erected at the request of foreign countries, are of western style.

Though the lighthouses at the beginning had been built, maintained and operated by western engineers, it did not take long before Japanese engineers became able to realize such constructions by themselves. The techniques acquired from the Westerners were improved to allow these buildings to resist earthquakes, which is very important in a country where everything is now done to protect buildings against seismic risks. The Japanese have also built many new lighthouses which they started maintaining and operating without external help.

Japan now has 67 historical lighthouses — more than one hundred years old — the aspect of which remains unchanged. The Japanese Maritime Safety Agency, who is responsible for these lighthouses, has defined a maintenance program in order to preserve them.

HIME-SAKI LIGHTHOUSE

Geographical Position:
Latitude 38°05'02" N
Longitude 138°33'57" E
Commissioned: 1895
Construction Material: Iron
Tower Height: 14.2 meters
Focal Plane Height: 41.5 meters

General: Hime-Saki lighthouse is the oldest iron lighthouse among those in operation in Japan.

Description: A hexagonal iron tower is painted white and originally housed a fourth-order lantern manufactured in 1895. In 1961 this lantern was upgraded to a revolving type LB-40 light. The optic produces a white flash of 50,000 candelas every 6 seconds. Electricity is supplied by commercial power with standby secondary batteries.

The structure of the lighthouse was reinforced by steel beams in 1994 as a result of investigations on its ability to withstand earthquakes in 1982 and 1991.

Inubo-Saki lighthouse

INUBO-SAKI LIGHTHOUSE

Geographical Position:
Latitude 35°42'52" N
Longitude 140°52'19" E
Commissioned: 1874
Architect: R. H. Brunton
Construction Material: Brick
Tower Height: 31.3 meters
Focal Plane Height: 52.3 meters

General: Inubo-Saki lighthouse is the oldest brick lighthouse among Japanese lighthouses in operation. The United States requested that Japan build a lighthouse at Cape Inubo to assist in navigating from Yokohama port (Japan) to North America.

Description: The cylindrical brick tower is painted white and originally housed a first-order lantern manufactured in 1874. The lantern was later upgraded to a first-order Fresnel lens rotating on a motor-driven mercury bath.

Bricks manufactured in Japan were of poor quality in those days. Discovery of good soil that could bear the weight of this light tower, and improvement in the manufacturing method, contributed to production of high-quality bricks comparable to those made in foreign countries.

The optic produces a white flash of 2,000,000 candelas every 15 seconds. Electricity is supplied by commercial power with a standby engine generator (6kVA). This lighthouse incorporates an aids to navigation office that administers the lighthouse, a fog signal station, a radio beacon station and a vessel traffic signal station.

Reinforcement with steel wires and pre-stressed concrete was carried out in 1986 as the result of an investigation on its ability to withstand earthquakes.

The lighthouse has been open to the public since 1948, and more than 210,000 people visit it each year.

IZUMO-HINOMISAKI LIGHTHOUSE

Geographical Position:
Latitude 35°25'51" N
Longitude 132°37'54" E
Commissioned: 1903
Architect: Ayahiko Ishibashi (Japanese engineer)
Construction Material: Stone (double wall with stone and brick)
Tower Height: 43.65 meters
Focal Plane Height: 63.3 meters

General: Izumo-Hinomisaki lighthouse is the highest stone lighthouse in Japan. This lighthouse was established in preparation for a possible increase in foreign trade with the opening of the port of Hamada and the port of Sakaiminato in Shimane prefecture. Both ports were opened in 1899 at the direction of the Meiji emperor.

Description: The white cylindrical stone tower contains a first-order lantern manufactured in 1898 and a first-order Fresnel lens manufactured in 1903. This lens rotates on a motor-driven mercury bath that was also manufactured in 1903. To improve its resistance to earthquakes the light tower uses a dual-material construction. Its outside wall is built of stone while its inner wall is constructed of brick.

The optic produces 2 group-flashing white lights and 2 group-flashing red lights of 460,000 candelas every 8 seconds. Electricity is supplied by commercial power with a standby generator (2kVA).

This lighthouse has been open to the public since 1948, and more than 180,000 people visit it each year.

MIHONOSEKI LIGHTHOUSE

Geographical Position:
Latitude 35°33'51" N
Longitude 133°19'41" E
Commissioned: 1898
Architect: Yoshitaka Kuroda (Japanese engineer)
Construction Material: Stone
Tower Height: 14 meters
Focal Plane Height: 82.91 meters

General: Mihonoseki lighthouse was established in preparation for a possible increase in foreign trade with the opening of the port of Hamada and the port of Sakaiminato in Shimane prefecture. Both ports were opened in 1899 at the direction of the Meiji emperor.

Description: The white cylindrical stone tower contains a first-order lantern, manufactured in 1898, and a revolving light type LBM-60 manufactured in 1992. The optic produces a white flash of 460,000 candelas every 12 seconds. Electricity is supplied by commercial power with a standby generator (2kVA).

Much care has been taken to preserve the historic look of the building. Now the old office and berthing serve as a restaurant.

Mihonoseki lighthouse

MIKOMOTO-SHIMA LIGHTHOUSE

Geographical Position:
Latitude 34°34'19" N
Longitude 138°56'41" E
Commissioned: 1870
Architect: R. H. Brunton
Construction Material: Stone
Tower Height: 23.31 meters
Focal Plane Height: 50.79 meters

General: Mikomoto-Shima lighthouse is the oldest stone lighthouse among Japanese lighthouses in operation. In 1866, the Edo Shogunate (former Japanese government) concluded a treaty (Edo Treaty) with the United States, the United Kingdom, the Netherlands, and France, which made Japan establish 8 lighthouses including the Mikomoto-Shima lighthouse. Commodore Perry, who visited Japan with an imposing fleet to urge the Edo Shogunate to open ports to foreign trade, recorded his difficulty in navigating around Mikomoto-Shima Island. The British Ambassador to Japan attended the opening ceremony in conjunction with high Japanese officials.

Description: The cylindrical stone tower is painted white with 2 horizontal black stripes. It contains a third-order Fresnel lens and a first-order lantern, both of which were manufactured in 1949. The dovetail method for fitting joints was used for the construction of the upper story of this tower, while cement was used for the vertical and horizontal joints in the middle and lower stories.

The optic produces 2 group-flashing white lights of 2,000,000 candelas every 16 seconds. Electricity is supplied by

3 generators (2kVA), manufactured in 1992. In 1982 and 1995, investigations on its ability to withstand earthquakes were carried out. Repairs were made each time by reinforcing the structure with carbon fiber, steel bars, and prestressed concrete. This island has been designated a site of national historical importance.

Macau

Lighthouse/Aids to Navigation Service of Macau

For many years, the coastal lighthouse (Guia) on the Macau Peninsula and two small lighthouses on Coloane Island have been guiding navigators.

Due to the heavy silting experienced in this region, buoyage systems and beacons also become very important. Only channels that are dredged and marked are guaranteed to have enough water for navigation. Macau has eight dredged channels with all the limits of these channels well marked by lighted buoys, lighted beacons, and unlighted buoys. All lighted buoys and beacons are equipped with modern lantern and solar power systems.

The Macau Harbor Master's office is responsible for the administration and maintenance of the aids to navigation in the Territory of Macau.

澳 門 港 務 局

GUIA LIGHTHOUSE

Geographical Position:
Latitude 22°11'51" N
Longitude 113°32'48" E
South China Sea
Date of building: 1865
Construction Material: Masonry
Tower Height: 16 meters
Focal Plane Height: 18 meters

Description: This is the oldest lighthouse on the China coast.

A white, cylindrical mansonry tower supports a lantern house with a revolving optic and 3 unequally spaced lens panels. The optic produces 2 flashes every 10 seconds and has a focal height of 18 meters. Electricity is supplied by the local electricity network. Originally it was lit by paraffin and later changed to electrical power in 1909. Beside the lighthouse, there is a post where signals are hoisted to warn of an approaching typhoon. In earlier times storm warnings were announced from the bell tower of the hermitage.

澳 門 港 務 局

Malaysia

PULAU UNDAN LIGHTHOUSE

Geographical Position:
Latitude 02°02'9" N
Longitude 102°20'1" E
Built: 1876
Main material: Masonry and wooden structure with an 8-sided tower

General: This lighthouse is believed to have been built by the Dutch. The color of the tower (red) is similar to the color of some of the old buildings built in the nearby historic city of Melaka during the Dutch era.

Description: The lighthouse is equipped with parabolic reflectors and 36 watt halogen lamps. These sit on a turntable with direct drive motors which give a light character of 2 flashes every 15 seconds and a range of 18 nautical miles. Photovoltaics are the power source for domestic and navigational light.

Singapore

HORSBURGH LIGHTHOUSE

Geographical Position:
Latitude 01°19'817" N
Longitude 104°24'444" E
South China Sea
Commissioned: 1851
Architect/Builder: J. T. Thomson
Construction Material: Granite
Tower Height: 29 meters
Focal Plane Height: 31 meters

General: Horsburgh Lighthouse is the oldest and most isolated among the 5 lighthouses of Singapore. The lighthouse was built on a lonely, rocky outcrop known as Pedra Branca (white rock) to mark the eastern approach to Singapore Strait from the South China Sea. Within the lighthouse vicinity are numerous, treacherous rocks and reefs where many ships were stranded and became easy prey for piracy, which was notorious prior to the construction of the lighthouse.

Horsburgh Lighthouse was designed and built by the government architect, J. T. Thomson and named after the late distinguished British hydrographer to the East India Company, Captain James Horsburgh. Construction of the lighthouse was financed by funds raised from a group of international merchants and mariners.

Description: The 29-meter white round tower with black bands supports a white lantern house.

Its original light source was from oil burners, but with progressive improvements over the years this was replaced with a multi-wick light source. This was housed in a dioptric first-order optic, and subsequently replaced by an incandescent vaporized kerosene burner. In 1966 the lighthouse was upgraded to electric power with a fourth-order optic and 1,000 watt light source. The light

intensity was increased by 3 times to 449,000 candelas with a light character flashing every 10 seconds. In 1988 the lighthouse operation was automated using solar energy.

PULAU PISANG LIGHTHOUSE

Geographical Position:
Latitude 01°28'167" N
Longitude 103°15'450" E
Malacca Strait
Commissioned: 1886
Construction Material: Brick and concrete
Tower Height: 18 meters
Focal Plane Height: 150 meters

General: Pulau Pisang Lighthouse was built in 1886 on top of a hill at Pulau Pisang in the Malacca Strait to mark the western approach to Singapore.

Description: The 18-meter white, round tower supports a white lantern house.

In 1967 the original first-order rotating optic with pressurized vapor burner equipment was replaced by a fourth-order 250 mm focus revolving lens. The new lens is electrically operated, producing an intensity of 615,000 candelas.

In 1986, Pulau Pisang Lighthouse was automated and powered by solar energy.

SULTAN SHOAL LIGHTHOUSE

Geographical Position:
Latitude 01°14'381" N
Longitude 103°38'985" E
Southwest of Singapore
Commissioned: 1896
Construction Material: Brick, concrete, and granite
Tower Height: 21 meters
Focal Plane Height: 20 meters

General: Sultan Shoal Lighthouse was erected in 1896 when the late Captain C.Q.D. Craufurd was the Master Attendant of Singapore. The lighthouse was built to replace the beacon which had marked the shoal earlier. Sultan Shoal Lighthouse was built on a concrete pillar erected on a submerged shoal.

Description: A two-story dwelling built around the 21-meter white, round tower supporting a white lantern house. The submerged shoal was reclaimed to an area of 10,000 square meters in 1975.

Its original light source was from 3 single-wick lamps fitted with parabolic reflectors. Over the years this was replaced with an incandescent oil dioptric light with Hood burner, used in a third-order 500 mm focus revolving optic, which revolved on mercury. This produced a light characteristic of group flashing twice every 15 seconds. In 1967 the incandescent kerosene Hood burning light equipment was replaced by an electrically operated 100 volt, 1,000 watt light source providing an intensity of 670,000 candelas and a range of 22 nautical miles.

In 1984, Sultan Shoal was automated and powered by solar energy.

RAFFLES LIGHTHOUSE

Geographical Position:
Latitude 01°09'609" N
Longitude 103°44'552" E
Main Strait of Singapore
Commissioned: 1855
Construction Material: Brick and granite
Tower Height: 29 meters
Focal Plane Height: 32 meters

General: Raffles Lighthouse was built in 1855 and named after Sir Stamford Raffles, the founder of modern Singapore. It was erected by the East India Company on Pulau Stumu, which is the southern tip of Singapore's territorial waters. The foundation stone was laid by Colonel W. J. Butterford C.B., the Governor of Straits Settlements. Though the island is rocky, it has a dense growth of coconut trees.

Description: The 29-meter white round tower supports a white lantern house.

Its original light source was a wick burner, which was replaced by a pressurized vapor kerosene mantle burner housed in a second-order optic to increase the light intensity for a greater visible range. In 1967 the second-order optic and machinery which had been operated efficiently for 112 years were replaced with an electrically driven fourth-order optic. The light source was changed to a 100 volt, 1,000 watt incandescent bulb producing 350,000 candelas of light intensity.

Subsequently in 1998 the lighthouse operation was automated using solar energy. The fourth-order optic was replaced with a PRB 24 lighting equipment comprising an array of quartz halogen lamps in aluminum parabolic reflectors mounted on a gearless revolving pedestal. The operation of the light is controlled by photo cell and time-switch, and its status is remotely monitored by a radio telemetry system.

Despite automation the lighthouse is manned by 2 crew members. Each crew is stationed at the offshore lighthouse for 16 days before returning to Singapore for shore leave, which is about 8 to 9 days. Crews are rotated to different lighthouses at 6-month intervals.

Vietnam

History

The Vietnam Maritime Safety Agency (VMS) is a state-run organization which is a subsidiary of the Vietnam National Maritime Bureau (VINAMARINE) and the Ministry of Transport (MOT).

The Vietnam Maritime Safety Agency has had its official name since the 1955 merging of the Office of Marine Safety (OMS) in the north and the Service of Maritime Safety (SMS) in the south.

The main functions of the VMS are:

• survey and design of the access channels to ports; dredging to ensure the depths of access channels; survey, amendment to coastal charts;

• design, manufacture, construction, and installation of aids to navigation of all kinds;

• responsibility for notices to mariners on channel depth, characteristics of aids to navigtion, etc.;

• administration, operation, and maintenance of aids to navigation to conform with Vietnamese Regulations and International Association of Lighthouse Authorities (IALA) recommendations;

• implementation of search and rescue and prevention of environmental pollution.

With a very skillful labor force and more than 40 years of operation, VMS has received many medals from the Vietnamese government.

In order to complete the Vietnamese lighthouse system, VMS is presently implementing its Project on Rehabilitation and Improvement of the Vietnamese Lighthouse System. This plan is estimated to be completed in 2010.

BAY CANH LIGHTHOUSE

Geographical Position:
Latitude 8°39'50" N
Longitude 106°46'36" E
East Sea — Pacific Ocean
Commissioned: 1885
Architect/Builder: French engineers,
Vietnamese builders
Construction Material: Stone, brick
Tower Height: 16 meters
Focal Plane Height: 212 meters
General: This is the oldest solidly constructed lighthouse of the Vietnamese lighthouse system, located on the water area of Ba Ria, Vung Tau province. It is a very important lighthouse for orientation and navigation in the region.

Description: A gray square masonry tower equipped with a rotating optical light (BBT-250 rotating beacon, France). The optic produces a flash of 1,000,000 candelas every 20 seconds and has a focal height of 212 meters. Diesel generators are used for the power source.

LONG CHAU LIGHTHOUSE

Geographical Position:
Latitude 20°37'24" N
Longitude 107°09'16" E
East Sea — Pacific Ocean
Commissioned: 1894
Architect/Builder: French engineers,
Vietnamese builders
Construction Material: Stone, brick
Tower Height: 30 meters
Focal Plane Height: 110 meters

General: This is the second oldest solidly constructed lighthouse. It plays a very important role in navigation observation in Bac Bo Gulf and is also a coastal station. This lighthouse is listed as a historical building.

Description: A gray cylindrical stone tower, equipped with a rotating beacon (PRB24) in June 1997. This gives a range of 28 nautical miles with a period of 15 seconds, and has a focal height of 110 meters. It is also equipped with a standby light HD500 (Vietnam) and radar beacon. Thirty two solar panels and 32 standby diesel generators are the power source.

E U R

O P E

Germany

History

In the 13th century the first daymarks and lights were established. They were operated and maintained on the German coasts by the individual ports without coordination. Over time this task was assumed without any coordination, by the German coastal states or the free ports, which in 1850 meant eight sovereign states. The German Nautical Association, which was founded in 1868, prepared at its first meeting a memorandum for the Parliament of the North German Confederation, which called for the improvement of the coastal lighting and the subordination of all off-shore aids to navigation to a central agency of the Confederation.

After the foundation of the German empire in 1871, on the initiative of some members of the Parliament, an amendment to the Constitution was achieved in 1874 to the effect that all aids to navigation were made subject to imperial supervision. The Imperial Navy was entrusted with the task of supervision, supported by a new civil aids to navigation organization.

By the new Constitution of the German Republic in 1919, the Central Government took possession of all aids to navigation, and they were now administered by the federal states on behalf of the Ministry of Transport.

Finally the Basic Law of 1949, which superseded the Constitution of 1919, provided that the navigable waterways including the aids to navigation, were not only owned by the Federal Government but that they were also administered by the Government through its own administrative authorities, the Waterway and Shipping Administration.

Thus, the date of 1949 marks for the Federal Republic of Germany the beginning of a uniform administration of the aids to navigation, within the Federal Ministry of Transport, the regional Waterways and Shipping Directorates and the local Waterways and Shipping Offices.

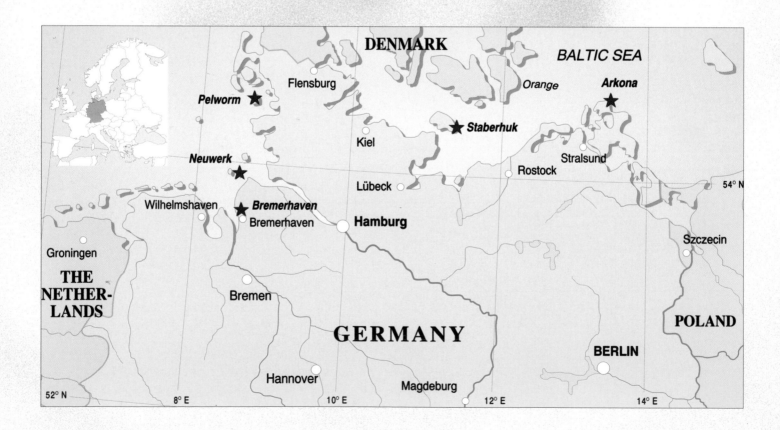

ARKONA LIGHTHOUSES

Geographical Position:
OLD LIGHTHOUSE (SWITCHED OFF):
Latitude 54°40'48" N
Longitude 13°26'04" E
NEW LIGHTHOUSE (IN OPERATION):
Latitude 54°40'47" N
Longitude 13°26'05" E
Baltic Sea
Building period:
OLD LIGHTHOUSE 1827
NEW LIGHTHOUSE 1902
Architect/Builder:
OLD LIGHTHOUSE: Karl Friedrich Schinkel
NEW LIGHTHOUSE: Unknown
Construction Material: Bricks
Tower Height:
OLD LIGHTHOUSE: 22.5 meters
NEW LIGHTHOUSE: 35 meters
Focal Plane Height:
NEW LIGHTHOUSE: 75 meters

General:
(Arkona lighthouses, old and new)
The old Arkona lighthouse was built to mark Cape Arkona, the northern point of Rügen Island. Because of increased nautical demands it was replaced in 1902 by the adjacent new Arkona lighthouse, still in operation.
Both are registered as historical buildings. Since 1995 the old lighthouse has been a maritime museum.
Description: (Old lighthouse) Square masonry tower unpainted, with one gallery and lantern with copper roof.
The optical system, now being reconstructed as a replica, consisted of 17, later 23, parabolic metal mirrors arranged in two rows, one above the other, f = 64 mm. Each mirror has a rapeseed oil lamp. They were later replaced by paraffin lamps.
Description: (New lighthouse) Conical masonry tower on octagonal granite base, unpainted, with two galleries and a red lantern, equipped with an optical system of three prismatic lenses on a common revolving pedestal, f = 22 mm. The optic produces a white flashing light with a 511,500 candelas effective intensity and a nominal range of 24 nautical miles. Electricity is supplied by the national grid with a standby diesel generator.

BREMERHAVEN LIGHTHOUSE

Geographical Position:
Latitude 53°32'49" N
Longitude 08°34'17" E
Weser River
Building year: 1854
Architect/Builder: Simon Loschen
Construction Material: Reddish brown bricks
Tower Height: 37.3 meters
Focal Plane Height: 34.9 meters

General: Around the city of Bremerhaven there is an interesting collection of 12 lighthouses, all of different design. The largest and oldest one is Bremerhaven Lighthouse, which was built in the neo-gothic style.
It is registered as a historical building.

Description: Together with the adjacent building which is also of neo-gothic design, the building slightly resembles a church. This is no coincidence; the lighthouse, including the house of the lock and lighthouse keepers, was designed by the architect Simon Loschen who also drew the plans for the main church in Bremerhaven. In former times a decorated iron crane jib was used to hoist storm-warning signals. These signals are nowadays transmitted by radio.
The optical system has been changed several times. First it consisted of 6 parabolic metal mirrors, diameter 28 cm. Each mirror had a rapeseed oil lamp.
In 1887 the optical system was replaced by a Mangin mirror, diameter 50 cm, and the energy supply was provided by gas.
Since 1925 the lighthouse has been equipped with a drum lens and operated electrically and since 1962 it has been remote-controlled. Even today it is still being used as the rear light of an alignment of lights extending upstream along the Weser River.
Electricity is supplied by the national grid with a standby diesel generator.

NEUWERK LIGHTHOUSE

Geographical Position:
Latitude 53°54'57" N
Longitude 08°29'49" E
North Sea
Building period: 1310
(lighthouse since 1814)
Construction Material: Bricks
Tower Height: 39 meters
Focal Plane Height: 38.7 meters

General: This is the oldest German lighthouse still in operation. Positioned on the island of Neuwerk off the Elbe estuary, it guides ships to Hamburg and has been a refuge for the islanders during storm surges ever since its construction. There are staterooms for officials and guests, as well as an inn, in the lighthouse. Visitors can go up to the first gallery. It is registered as a historical building.

Description: Square masonry tower unpainted on foundation of boulders, with two galleries and a copper lantern, equipped with a drum lens, manufactured in 1892, f = 700 mm. The optic produces a light flashing white, red and green with a 19,300 candelas effective intensity and a nominal range of 16 nautical miles. Electricity is produced by the national grid with a standby diesel generator.

PELLWORM LIGHTHOUSE

Geographical Position:
Latitude 54°29'49" N
Longitude 08°40'02" E
North Sea
Building year: 1907
Architect/Builder: Isselburger Hütte (manufacturer)
Construction Material: cast iron
Tower Height: 41.5 meters
Focal Plane Height: 37.8 meters

General: This lighthouse is one of several cast iron lighthouses in Germany. It marks the fairways to some North Frisian islands and to the Port of Husum. It now houses three independent lights, and is equipped with a sophisticated optical system. It is registered as a historical building.

Description: Conical tower, made of cast iron elements bolted together on site, on a brick foundation and with two galleries, painted red with a white horizontal band and a black lantern, equipped with:

1. Rear light of Pellworm leading lights: spherical metal mirror; prismatic lens, 7 prisms; vertical spread lenses; manufactured in 1907.

2. Süderaue sector light: prismatic reinforcing mirror and drum lens manufactured in 1931.

3. Ochsensand sector light: drum lens. Electricity is supplied by the national grid with a standby diesel generator.

STABERHUK LIGHTHOUSE

Geographical Position:
Latitude 54°24'11" N
Longitude 11°18'43" E
Baltic Sea
Building period: 1903
Construction Material: Bricks
Tower Height: 22.6 meters
Focal Plane Height: 25.5 meters

General: This lighthouse marks the south-eastern point of Fehmarn Island. The lantern and optical system come from a very similar, older lighthouse built by the Trinity House Corporation, England, in 1811 on Helgoland Island (North Sea). In 1902 the Helgoland light was replaced by a new one with a higher focal plane and a longer range. The lighthouse is registered as a historical building.

Description: Conical masonry tower unpainted, with a red lantern, equipped with a drum lens, manufactured about 1875 in England by Chance Brothers for the Trinity House Corporation, diameter 925 mm, revolving screens.

The optic produces a light flashing white and green with a 70,000 candelas effective intensity and a nominal range of 18 nautical miles. Electricity is supplied by the national grid with a standby diesel generator.

England

Trinity House Lighthouse Service

History/Responsibility

The Corporation of Trinity House was first empowered to erect seamarks by Queen Elizabeth I under the provisions of the Seamarks Act 1566. In 1594 the Lord High Admiral surrendered to Her Majesty the rights of beaconage and buoyage vested in him with the recommendation, which was adopted, that these be bestowed upon Trinity House.

The first lighthouse built by Trinity House was at Lowestoft in 1609. A long interval elapsed before the Corporation became responsible for the management of all lighthouses due to the continued practice of the Crown issuing patents or grants of lighthouses to private individuals who, on payment of a rent, had the right to collect tolls for the use of particular lights. These private lights varied in efficiency and in 1836 Trinity House was given compulsory powers to buy out the private individuals who owned the lights and to maintain them itself.

The Corporation of Trinity House has three main roles:

• the General Lighthouse Authority for England, Wales, and the Channel Islands (Trinity House Lighthouse Service);

• a charitable organization for the safety, welfare, and training of mariners and the relief of those who are in financial distress;

• a Deep Sea Pilotage Authority.

Trinity House Lighthouse Service is responsible for visual and audible fixed and floating seamarks, plus electronic aids to navigation including the Decca Navigator System, radio beacons and racons. The Service maintains 72 lighthouses, of which 7 are manned, and 22 beacons.

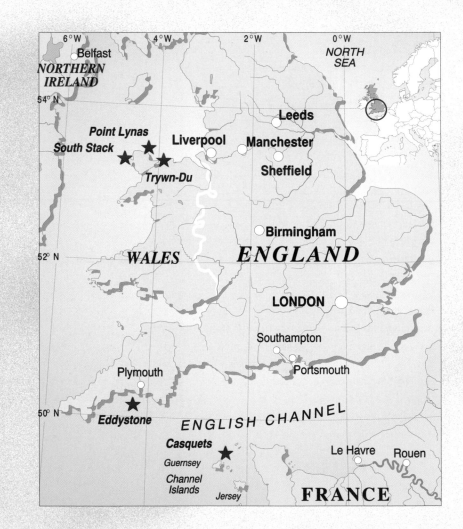

CASQUETS LIGHTHOUSE

Geographical Position:
Latitude 49°43'24" N
Longitude 02°22'42" W
English Channel off Guernsey
Commissioned: 1723-1724
Architect/Builder: Designed by William Norman and erected by Thomas Le Cocq
Construction Material: Masonry
Tower Height: 23 meters
Focal Plane Height: 37 meters

General: In about 1722 the owners of ships passing certain dangerous rocks called the Casketts off Alderney in the Channel Islands applied to Thomas Le Cocq, the owner of the rocks, to build a lighthouse. They offered him payment based on tonnage when vessels passed the light.

Trinity House decided that a light of particular character to distinguish it from those on the opposite shores of England and France was needed. Three separate lights in the form of a horizontal triangle were proposed, each displaying coal fires within lanterns. These three lights, called St. Peter, St. Thomas, and Dudgeon Towers, were first exhibited on October 30, 1724. The

three lights were changed to metal reflectors and Argand lamps in 1790 and a revolving apparatus was installed in 1818. The station was electrified in 1952 and today only St. Peter Tower exhibits a light. The keepers were removed from the station in 1990 upon automation of the station.

Description: The station consists of three towers, surrounding a courtyard approximately 14-meters above high water mark. Between St. Peter and Dudgeon Towers, a single-story keeper's accommodation is built with pitched slate roof. The building and towers are built from random stone rendered externally. Dudgeon Tower was once used as an engine room and supported the air fog signal. This has since been abandoned, with the engines now located in the base of St. Thomas Tower. On top, a helipad has been constructed.

The light source is a 400 watt MBI lamp within a second-order 700 mm five-panel lens floating on a mercury bath, giving 5 white flashes every 30 seconds, 1,079,000 candelas, 24 sea miles range. An electric fog signal gives 2 blasts every 60 seconds with a range of 3 sea miles.

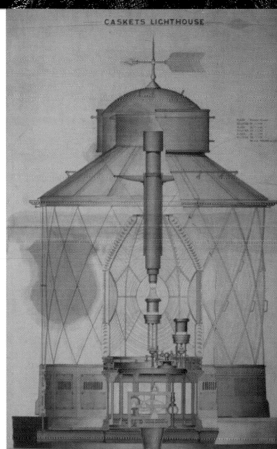

CASKETS LIGHTHOUSE

EDDYSTONE LIGHTHOUSE

Geographical Position:
Latitude 50°10'48" N
Longitude 04°15'69" W
English Channel
Commissioned: 1882, latest in
a succession of four separate lighthouses
beginning in 1698
Architect/Builder: James Douglass
Construction Material: Granite
Tower Height: 49 meters
Focal Plane Height: 41 meters

General: The most famous lighthouse in the British Isles is probably the Eddystone, built on a small and very dangerous rock, 13 miles southwest of Plymouth.

There have been four separate lighthouses built there. The original tower was completed in 1698 by Winstanley and was the first lighthouse to be built on a small rock in the open sea. In 1703 during a severe storm the tower and occupants were lost.

The second, constructed of wood, was built by John Rudyard in 1709 and served for 47 years until on December 2, 1755, the lantern caught fire and spread to the rest of the structure.

John Smeaton designed and built the next tower in 1759 constructed from interlocking granite blocks. Its design was so successful that it stood for over 120 years when finally the rock upon which it stood became undermined by a cave and the upper section was dismantled and erected on shore at Plymouth in 1882. The current tower was built on an adjacent rock and completed in 1882.

Description: A 49-meter circular granite tower, solid at its base for the first 12 meters. Boat landings can be made onto the offset and then access is by dog steps up to the entrance door. The tower has 9 levels below the lantern. Above the lantern a steel/aluminum helicopter landing pad was added in 1980. A fourth-order, four-panel catadioptric lens with a 70 watt MBI lamp provides a range of 20 sea miles.

The optic is rotated by an AGA PRB20 gearless pedestal.

The station was automated in 1982 and operates on a 24 hour 240 volt AC generating system. The station has a 6 kw nautophone fog signal.

EDDYSTONE PROPOSED NEW LIGHTHOUSE

POINT LYNAS LIGHTHOUSE

Geographical Position:
Latitude 52°25'00" N
Longitude 04°17'18" W
North Coast of Anglesey
Commissioned: 1835
Architect/Builder: Jesse Hartley, engineer
to Mersey Docks and Harbour Board
Construction Material: Masonry
Tower Height: 11 meters
Focal Plane Height: 39 meters

General: As early as 1766 the need was felt for a station on Anglesey where ships making for Liverpool could pick up pilots. At first the early pilots used a farmhouse as their lookout post. The lighthouse was built in 1835 by the Mersey Docks and Harbour Board. In 1879 a telegraph station was established and the site extended to include two additional cottages and the boundary wall extended to encompass the whole site. Entry to the site is via gates below a stilted archway. The boundary wall is castellated. The original wall along the north elevation has an inner wall-walk carried on recessed arches. This latter work was designed by George Lyster. The lighthouse was electrified in 1952 and Trinity House took over responsibility for the light in 1973. The station was automated in 1992.

The lighthouse is an important work of Jesse Hartley, with Lyster's extension maintaining a similar character. The design bears a distinctive hallmark and is quite different from those associated with Trinity House. This distinctive exercise in neo-gothic forms a tightly designed and highly integrated compound. The lighthouse is of an unusual type in which the lantern is on the ground floor.

Description : The lighthouse is set to the rear of the Principal Keeper's cottage, white rendered over rubble, a rectangular tower with a higher and narrow tower at its north end housing the telegraph room and lookout in its upper floor. The lantern projects from the north elevation at ground level. The semicir-

cular cast iron lantern is carried on a wide masonry platform enclosed by a ditch.

The second-order 1400 mm catadioptric fixed lens dates from 1879 and has an occulting character of white every 10 seconds with a range of 20 sea miles.

SOUTH STACK LIGHTHOUSE

Geographical Position:
Latitude 53°18'24" N
Longitude 04°41'54" W
Off Holyhead Island, Anglesey,
North Wales
Commissioned: 1809
Architect/Builder: Alexander
Construction Material: Masonry
Tower Height: 28 meters
Focal Plane Height: 60 meters

General: South Stack Lighthouse was first envisaged in 1665 when a petition for a patent to erect the lighthouse was presented to Charles II. The patent was not granted and it was not until February 9, 1809, that the first light appeared to mark the rock. The lighthouse was designed by Alexander and originally fitted with Argand oil lamps and reflectors. Around 1840 a railway was installed by means of which a lantern with a subsidiary light could be lowered down the cliff to sea level when fog obscured the main light. The chasm between the mainland and the rock was at first traversed by a hempen cable 21 meters above sea level, along which a sliding basket was drawn carrying a passenger or stores. This system of conveyance was replaced in 1828 by an iron suspension bridge 1.5 meters wide, and again in 1964 by the present aluminum bridge. The landward approach to the bridge is by descending 400 steps cut into the cliff face.

In the mid 1870s the lantern and lighting apparatus were replaced by a new lantern. No records are available of the light source at this time but it was probably a pressurized multiwick oil lamp. In 1909 an early form of incandescent light was installed and in 1927 this was replaced by a more modern form of incandescent mantle burner. The station was electrified in 1938. The station was automated in September 1984 and the keepers withdrawn.

Description: The station consists of a traditionally designed tower 28 meters high with first-order catadioptric rotating lens in a mercury bath. The lens is first order, 920 mm in focal length, consisting of six panels giving a white flash every 10 seconds. The light source is a 1 kw MBI lamp providing a range of 23 sea miles.

A fog signal emitter stack is situated in front of the lighthouse.

A single-story engine room and keeper's accommodation block connects with the base of the tower. The slate roof is formed of two pitches with valley gutter between.

TRWYN-DU LIGHTHOUSE

Geographical Position:
Latitude 53°18'48" N
Longitude 04°02'24" W
Off the Island of Anglesey at the entrance to the Menai Strait
Commissioned: 1838
Architect/Builder: James Walker
Construction Material: Granite
Tower Height: 29 meters
Focal Plane Height: 19 meters

General: The lighthouse is situated in the strait between Penmon Point, Anglesey, and Puffin Island, close to the shore but accessible at low tide. The lighthouse was built to mark the north entrance to Menai Strait and the passage between the two islands. It was designed by James Walker, consultant engineer to Trinity House. The lighthouse was manned until 1992 when it was automated and converted to acetylene gas. Originally connected to the shore by a cast iron bridge, it has remained virtually untouched since that date and special care was taken during the solar conversion of the station in 1995.

Description: Ashlar stone, painted in broad bands of black and white. Stepped circular tower up to halfway point with crenellated parapet corbelled out; cast iron lantern with conical roof surmounted by ball finial carrying arrow weather vane. All windows are small-paned sashes, the openings apparently originally triple-glazed.

The station was solarized in 1995 with the solar module mounting frame supported off the gallery in the blanc arc. The carbon dioxide gas fog bell was converted to electric operation using a stepper motor drive system. The light is provided by an ML300 beacon mounted outside the lantern providing a range of 12 sea miles.

SUŠAC LIGHTHOUSE

Geographical Position:
Latitude 42°45'0" N
Longitude 16°29'7" E
Commissioned: 1878
Construction Material: Massive stone
Tower Height: 17 meters
Focal Plane Height: 94 meters

General: Sušac lighthouse is situated on the southwest side of the island bearing the same name, on the west side of the Channel of Lastovo. It is utilized for navigation along the central Adriatic route and also as a bifurcation towards the ports of Central Dalmatia.

Description: Sušac lighthouse consists of a square stone tower situated over a stone lantern house. Lighting equipment uses mechanical revolving optic with a light range of 24 nautical miles (47,000 candelas). It is powered by batteries and a generator. It is also equipped with a standby solar light that has a range of 12 nautical miles.

SAVUDRIJA LIGHTHOUSE

Geographical Position:
Latitude 45°29'4" N
Longitude 13°29'5" E
Commissioned: 1818
Construction Material: Stone/concrete
Tower Height: 29 meters
Focal Plane Height: 36 meters

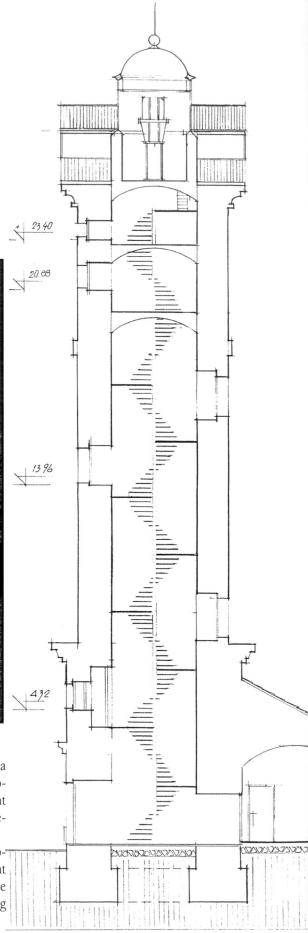

General: Savudrija lighthouse is the oldest lighthouse on the Croatian coast of the Adriatic Sea. It is situated on the westernmost cape of the Istrian peninsula bearing the same name. Apart from being used for navigation towards the western ports of Istria, it is essential in navigating towards the Slovenian port of Koper and Italian port of Trieste.

Description: Savudrija lighthouse consists of a stone tower with gallery and concrete cupola. Lighting equipment consists of a revolving beacon PRB-20 with optic supplied by mains electricity, with a light range of 30 nautical miles (27,000 candelas).

It also has a standby light with catadioptric lens and automatic supply with a light range of 12 nautical miles. The lighthouse is also equipped with an electrical fog signal.

PALAGRUZA LIGHTHOUSE

Geographical Position:
Latitude 42°23'5" N
Longitude 16°15'6" E
Commissioned: 1875
Construction Material: Massive stone
Tower Height: 22 meters
Focal Plane Height: 110 meters

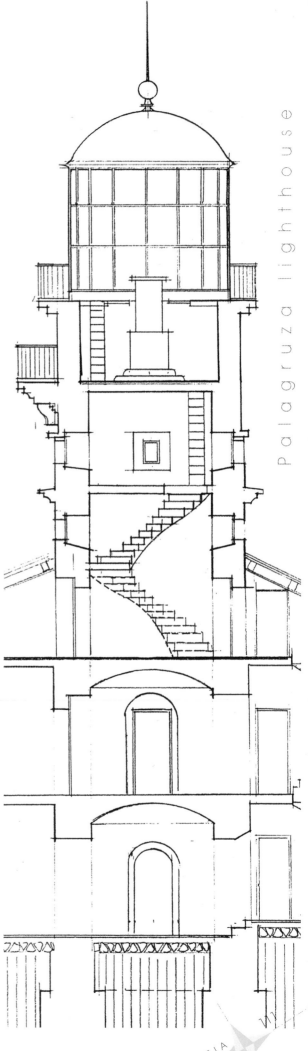

General: Palagruza lighthouse is the biggest and the most distant lighthouse of the Republic of Croatia. It is located on the island of Vela Palagruza, making part of an archipelago bearing the same name and it is situated in the central part of the Adriatic Sea, between the Italian and the Croatian coasts. This lighthouse is the first to be encountered when navigating from Oranto towards the Adriatic ports.

Description: Palagruza lighthouse consists of a stone tower situated above a stone lantern house. Lighting equipment consists of a revolving beacon with optic. It is powered by batteries filled by a generator. Light range is 26 nautical miles (79,000 candelas). The lighthouse is also equipped with a standby solar light having a range of 12 nautical miles. This lighthouse has also been an important meteorological station for more than 100 years.

PORER LIGHTHOUSE

Geographical Position:
Latitude 44°45'5" N
Longitude 13°53'8" E
Commissioned: 1833
Construction Material: Massive stone
Tower Height: 31 meters
Focal Plane Height: 35 meters

General: Porer lighthouse is situated on a bare cliff having a round shape, with a diameter of only 80 meters, 1 mile to the southwest of the southernmost cape of the Istrian peninsula. It is very useful for navigating towards the northern Adriatic ports and also as a bifurcation for the ports in the Gulf of Kvarner.

Description: Porer lighthouse consists of a stone tower making part of a stone lantern house. Its main light consists of a revolving beacon P5B-20 with optic, supplied by mains electricity, with a light range of 25 nautical miles (70,000 candelas).
The lighthouse is also equipped with a notophone and a fog detector. The whole building is protected with Chem-rod lightning protection.

ISLE OF MAY LIGHTHOUSE

Geographical Position:
Latitude 56°11'2" N
Longitude 02°33'3" W
North Sea
Commissioned: 1816
Architect/Builder:
Robert Stevenson
Construction Material: Lower building,
course brick with dressed stone corner
bands, dressed sandstone corbelling
parapets. Square Tower,
dressed sandstone.
Tower Height: 24 meters
Focal Plane Height: 73 meters

General: The lighthouse building is listed
as a building of architectural and historical
interest.
The Isle of May was the site of Scotland's
earliest coal-fired light, established in
1636. The original tower remains today.
The Isle of May was automated in 1989
and is now remotely monitored from the
Northern Lighthouse Board's headquarters
in Edinburgh.

Description : The square gothic tower
stands on a stone dwelling. The optic is a
sealed beam lamp array which produces
2 flashes of 269,280 candelas every
15 seconds and has a range of 22 miles.

SKERRYVORE LIGHTHOUSE

Geographical Position:
Latitude 56°19'4" N
Longitude 07°06'9" W
Atlantic Ocean
Commissioned: 1844
Architect/Builder: Alan Stevenson
Construction Material: Gray granite
Tower Height: 48 meters
Focal Plane Height: 46 meters

General: Skerryvore is the tallest Scottish lighthouse and it has been said to be the world's most graceful lighthouse.
Skerryvore was automated in 1994 and is now remotely monitored from the Northern Lighthouse Board's headquarters in Edinburgh.
Description: Skerryvore is a 48-meter pillar rock lighthouse of gray granite built on a treacherous submerged reef of rocks. The optic, a fourth-order catadioptric rotating system comprising three panels, produces a flash of 366,000 candelas every 10 seconds and has a range of 23 miles.

BELL ROCK LIGHTHOUSE

Geographical Position:
Latitude 56°26'1" N
Longitude 02°23'1" W
North Sea
Commissioned: 1811
Architect/Builder: Robert Stevenson
Construction Material: Stone
Tower Height: 36 meters
Focal Plane Height: 28 meters

General: The Bell Rock is the oldest rock lighthouse in the British Isles.
The Bell Rock was automated in 1988 and is now remotely monitored from the Northern Lighthouse Board's headquarters in Edinburgh.

Description: The Bell Rock is a pillar rock lighthouse built on a treacherous submerged reef in the North Sea. The optic, a fourth-order catadioptric rotating system comprising four panels, produces a flash of 55,000 candelas every 5 seconds and has a range of 18 miles.

Spain

History and responsibility

The Service, with a nationwide scope, was established in 1842 and it has always been dependent on a Director General of the Ministry in charge of ports and coasts. For more than a century and a half it has consisted of a central organ in the Ministry and peripheral services in all the coastal provinces.

The first National Plan of Lighthouses dates from 1847. The Plan included 143 lighthouses and 362 beacons, buoys, etc. in the Peninsula and the Balearic Islands. Subsequent plans also included the Canary Islands, the territories in Africa and America belonging to the Spanish Crown, and the Philippines.

The Spanish Constitution (1978) provides that the State has exclusive responsibility over coastal lighting, maritime signaling and ports of general interest. On January 1, 1993, the traditional status was modified to shift responsibility to the Ministry of Public Works, Transports and the Environment through its port organ Puertos del Estado (State Ports of Spain) and the 27 Port Authorities.

At present the Port Authorities are responsible for the local management of 191 lighthouses and 1,023 visual, audible and radio electrical aids to navigation. They also are responsible for the inspection of the 891 aids managed by the Regional Governments, Municipalities, etc. Puertos del Estado, for its part, has to plan, harmonize, control and define the aids to navigation throughout the country.

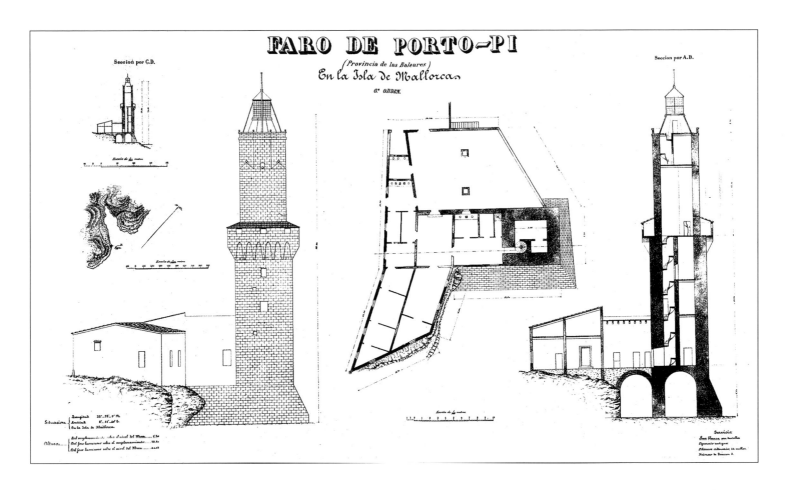

FARO DE PORTO-PI

(Provincia de las Baleares)

En la Isla De Mallorcas

6ª ORDEN.

Seccion por C.D.

Seccion por A.B.

PORTO PI LIGHTHOUSE

Geographical Position:
Latitude 39°33'0" N
Longitude 02°37'5" W
Mediterranean Sea
Construction date: 1290
Construction Material: Brownish-gray stone
Tower Height: 38 meters
Focal Plane Height: 41 meters

General: This lighthouse is located in Majorca, one of the Balearic Islands, and is one of the oldest lighthouses in Spain. It was originally installed over one of the towers built in the 13th century under the reign of James II. During the 17th century, a fort was built in order to defend the city from Berber attacks and from which the arrival of the enemy was greeted with heavy cannon fire. Vibrations from the can-

non fire broke the glass in the lantern, so the lighthouse was moved to the present Signal Tower. The signal tower was constructed in the same period as the primitive tower. From this position, the lighthouse keeper could see the number of enemy boats approaching from any direction and use a signal system consisting of flags of different colors and shapes located at the top of the tower.

The light first worked on olive oil, which pupils of the Majorca College of Merchandise were responsible for replenishing. The olive oil was substituted with paraffin, later with petrol, and finally electricity was installed. During the 19th century a revolving optic was installed. This equipment was made up of 14 lamps around which 3 parabolic mirrors turned, covered by a glass lantern with a wooden structure.

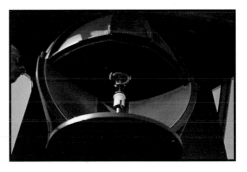

The lighthouse is now completely automated and continues to work as a navigational aid. It is also home to a small museum. On August 14, 1983, it was declared a National Historic Artistic Monument.

Description: Square tower of brownish-gray stone, 38 meters high and equipped with a catoptric optic of 4 parabolic reflectors which revolves on ball bearings around a 1,000 watt lamp. The light emitted is white and flashes twice every 15 seconds. Its nominal range is 22 nautical miles.

Torre

THE TOWER OF HERCULES LIGHTHOUSE

Geographical Position:
Latitude 43°23'2" N
Longitude 08°24'3" W
Atlantic Ocean
Construction date: 2nd century,
Trajan period
Architect/Builder: Reconstructed by
Eustaquio Giannini
Construction Material: Granite masonry
Tower Height: 49 meters
Focal Plane Height: 106 meters

General: This lighthouse is situated upon a hillock on the Galician coast just outside the city of La Coru. Legend attributes the origins of this primitive construction to the battle between Hercules and the Giant Gerion. Victorious, Hercules had the bones of this enemy buried in the foundations of the tower which he had built there. As tradition would have it, the Tower of Hercules is over 3,000 years old. In this time it is said that it was left in ruins and rebuilt on several occasions. Both the Welsh and the Scots have legends about the lighthouse of Brigantia. The Scots talk of how the lighthouse rock was stolen by Cathol, King of Scotland.

Engraved in a small rock at the foot of the tower is an inscription in Latin which is considered to be key to the determining of the period of the construction. The inscription is as follows: "Dedicated to Marte Augustus, Cayo Servio Lupo, architect of Aeminium in Lusitania, in accordance with his oath." It is generally accepted that the lighthouse was constructed in the second century A.D. under the Emperor Trajan.

The first precise geographical reference can be found in Ptolemy's "Greco-Latin Geography." The first known written comment about this lighthouse is one by Dion Casio (third century), who describes how a fleet commanded by Julius Caesar weighed anchor at its feet. At the beginning of the fifth century, Orosio speaks of the lighthouse like an old fort which at that time

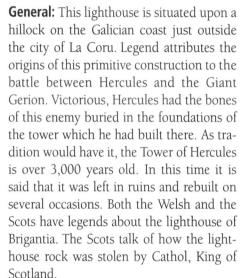

was half destroyed, and explains how its light had been so useful for the security and orientation of Roman expeditions to Brittany.

The Bishop Sebastiano explains how in the year 844 the Normans invaded Gijon, "from whence they swept through to a place called Farum Brigantium." The archbishop Rodrigo, narrating the same story on another occasion, calls it the Lighthouse of Galicia, indicating its use as a light. The map drawn up in Burgo de Osma (1086) contains the lighthouses of Alexandria and the Tower of Hercules.

Throughout the 15th and 16th centuries, family feuds and attacks on the City of La Coru by Francis Drake left little more than four walls standing in the lighthouse. Threatened with complete collapse due to the damage incurred and the fact that materials from it were being used in other constructions, the City Council, in 1553, decided to prohibit the latter activity. The repair of the lighthouse was not seriously considered until 1684, when Adrian of Roo, Consul of Flanders, proposed to the Duke of Uceda that a wooden ladder be erected in order to reach the upper floors and that two stone turrets be constructed in order to put a lamp on each one. Adrian of Roo was arrested for failing to meet the conditions laid down in the contract, and another person was appointed to light the lamps. This service did not, however, last very long; the lamps went out, the stairway collapsed and the tower returned to its previous state of ruin.

The definitive solution to this situation came in 1785 when King Charles III created the Maritime Consulate of Galicia, which, in its first actions asked the Marine Council of the Ferrol Department to assign an engineer to the job of reconstructing the tower. In accordance with the plans and under the direction of Eustaquio Giannini, Marine Lieutenant, the building rose again with an octagonal trunk. The outer walls were covered with a 60-cm thickness of

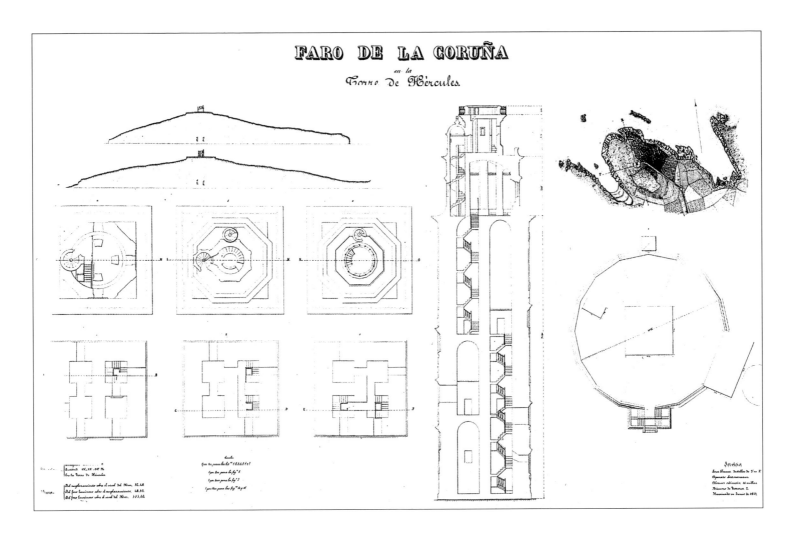

FARO DE LA CORUÑA
en la
Torre De Hércules

granite, a stairway was built inside the tower, and in the upper section, a lantern was placed. The reconstruction work was completed in 1790.

The magnificent result was what we can now see today. Since then the only noteworthy changes have been those of a technological nature affecting the lighting system which, according to Giannini's original idea, consisted of a revolving light based on a coal fire. However, when the work was finished, it was changed for seven oil lights whose eclipses were made by moving iron plates by means of a clockwork mechanism. In 1847, the lighting mechanism was made up of a revolving system with 11 large reflectors, 11 small reflectors and 12 convex lenses with olive oil lamps. In 1883, the tower had a Letourneau equipment with a dual wick mechanical

L. Sautter lamp powered by Scottish paraffin. In 1904, an incandescent petroleum vapor lamp was installed, also from Sautter in Paris. Finally, in 1921 the electrification of the lighthouse was completed. More recently, a radio beacon has been installed, together with a siren and other small-scale aesthetic reforms.

Description: Square masonry tower with an octagonal upper part, 49 meters high. It is equipped with a revolving dioptric catadioptric optic with an electrical 1,500 watt bulb and a focal plane height of 106 meters. The light emitted is white and consists of 4 flashes every 20 seconds with a nominal range of 23 nautical miles.

De

Hércules.

THE CABO MAYOR LIGHTHOUSE

Geographical Position:
Latitude 43°29'5" N
Longitude 03°47'4" W
Cantabrian Sea
Commissioned: 1839
Architect/Builder: Domingo Rogi
Construction Material: Masonry
Tower Height: 30 meters
Focal Plane Height: 91 meters

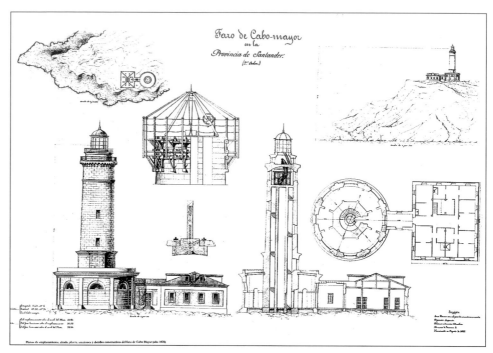

General: In 1776 traders were clamoring for a lighthouse to be provided at the mouth of the Port of Santander. The project was not carried out, however, until some 60 years later. The optic was made up of 8 lenses and had 100 upper mirrors and 60 lower mirrors. The lamp was originally an oil burner with 3 concentric wicks. Today the lighthouse is a symbol of the city as well as a tourist attraction. Its extensive premises are open to the public during the day.

Description: Cylindrical, gray stone tower, 30 meters high. The lighting system produces a white light and gives out 2 flashes in a 10 second period. The height of the focal plane is 91 meters giving the lighthouse a nominal range of 21 nautical miles. It is equipped with a BBT 375 mm bivalve optic floating on a mercury tank.

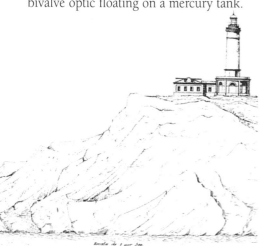

CABO DE PALOS LIGHTHOUSE

Geographical Position:
Latitude 37°38'2" N
Longitude 0°41'3" W
Mediterranean Sea
Architect/Builder: Evaristo Churruca
Construction Material: Granite masonry
Tower Height: 51 meters
Focal Plane Height: 81 meters

General: This lighthouse was included in the first Plan of Illumination of Spanish coasts of 1847 and was set to be the home of the School of Lighthouses which would train candidates for the Corps of Lighthousemen. The construction consists of a square, two-story building on which the tower is built. This tower has a first stage which is octagonal in shape and a second stage which is a slightly conical stonework column. The rotating optic and the polygonal lantern originally installed came from Lepaute of Paris. The lamp was first powered by olive oil, later by paraffin and petrol. It was finally electrified in 1960.

Description: A slightly conical tower 51 meters high and gray in color. The lighting system produces a white light which flashes twice every 10 seconds. The height of the focal plane is 81 meters and its nominal range is 23 nautical miles. At the present time, it has a revolving dioptric lighting system with two 1,500 watt lamps and a V automatic lamp changer.

THE CASTRO URDIALES LIGHTHOUSE

Geographical Position:
Latitude 43°23'1" N
Longitude 03°12'9" W
Cantabrian Sea
Construction Date: 18th century
Construction Material: Masonry
Tower Height: 16 meters
Focal Plane Height: 49 meters

General: The tower is constructed upon the southeast tower of the Castle of Ste Anne, dating back to the 13th century. The old chapel is now the engine room. The first oil lamp was installed in 1853. In 1919 it was electrified and it now has a revolving reflector optic with sealed beam lamps floating on a mercury tank. There is a project to turn the castle into a museum and to build a hut on the existing site to house the engine room without spoiling the overall harmony of this group of buildings.
Description: A 16-meter-high tower, conical in shape and painted white. Light consists of 4 white light flashes in 24 seconds. Its nominal range is 20 nautical miles.

FARO DE CASTRO URDIALES
en la
Provincia de Santander

Thanks : Ministerio de Obras Públicas y Urbanismo - M.A. Sánchez Terry - *Faros españoles del Océano* - 1987
Ministerio de Obras Públicas y Urbanismo - M.A Sánchez Terry - *Faros españoles del Mediterranéo* - 1987
Paisajes Españoles, S.A.
Autoridad Portuaria de Baleares
Autoridad Portuaria de La Coruña
Autoridad Porturaria de Santander.

Estonia

History

The Estonian National Maritime Board (ENMB, national maritime administration in Estonia) was re-established in April 1990, one year before Estonia officially regained its independence. ENMB is responsible for the safety of navigation in Estonian waters, including aids to navigation and hydrography. The actual work of maintaining the aids to navigation started in the autumn of 1993 when the Russian Navy handed over all aids to navigation in Estonian waters to ENMB. In Estonian waters (including inner waters) there are 1,150 aids to navigation of various kinds, including 58 lighthouses.

As of 1997 ENMB employs 450 people, of which 350 work for the lighthouse and hydrographic service. Ten of the lighthouses were built before 1800 and two-thirds of them before the 20th century; 20 of the lighthouses are manned today. The number of manned lighthouses is diminishing substantially in accordance with the modernization and automation of lighthouses connected to a common monitoring system. Many of the old lighthouses are unique and of architectural value. The evaluation of their historical value is under way.

KOPU LIGHTHOUSE

Geographical Position:
Latitude 58°54'96" N
Longitude 22°11'98" E
Commissioned: 1531
Architect/Builder: Hans Scherer
and Klaves Duker
Construction Material: Limestone
Tower Height: 36 meters
Focal Plane Height: 102 meters

General: This lighthouse is under government protection as a national monument. It is very massive and of unique construction.

Description: White quadrangular stone tower with retaining walls and red lantern room, and viewing platform. It operates with a revolving lens and has a range of 26 miles.

PAKRI LIGHTHOUSE

Geographical Position:
Latitude 59°23'25" N
Longitude 24°02'26" E
Commissioned: 1889
(1724, original lighthouse)
Construction Material: Stone
Tower Height: 52 meters
Focal Plane Height: 73 meters

General: This is one of the highest historical lighthouses on the Baltic Sea.

Description: Red cylindrical brick tower with gallery and lantern room. It works on mains power, and is fully automated and connected to the common monitoring system.

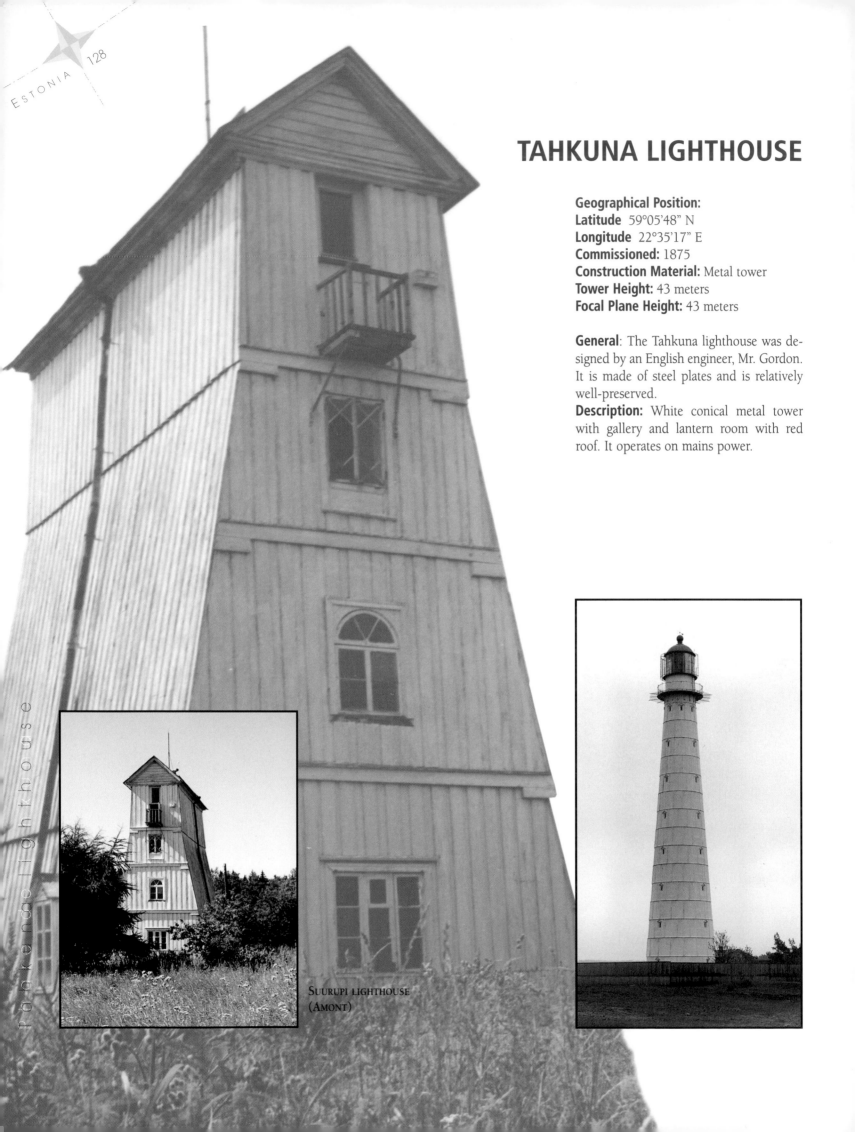

Pakkage lighthouse

TAHKUNA LIGHTHOUSE

Geographical Position:
Latitude 59°05'48" N
Longitude 22°35'17" E
Commissioned: 1875
Construction Material: Metal tower
Tower Height: 43 meters
Focal Plane Height: 43 meters

General: The Tahkuna lighthouse was designed by an English engineer, Mr. Gordon. It is made of steel plates and is relatively well-preserved.
Description: White conical metal tower with gallery and lantern room with red roof. It operates on mains power.

SUURUPI LIGHTHOUSE
(AMONT)

KERI LIGHTHOUSE

Geographical Position:
Latitude 59°41'93" N
Longitude 25°01'37" E
Commissioned: 1719
Construction Material:
Metal tower and stone base
Tower Height: 31 meters
Focal Plane Height: 31 meters

General: This lighthouse was declared a national monument in 1996. It has a unique bottle shape construction, with the northern wall badly damaged. The lighthouse is temporarily preserved.

Description: Red cylindrical metal tower with gallery and lantern room on stone base. It operates on solar power and a wind generator. It is controlled by a communication controller which is connected to the

RUHNU LIGHTHOUSE

Geographical Position:
Latitude 57°48'09" N
Longitude 23°15'62" E
Commissioned: Unknown
(1646, original lighthouse)
Construction Material: Metal tower
Tower Height: 40 meters
Focal Plane Height: 65 meters

General: The present lighthouse was erected in 1877 in place of a wooden lighthouse, which was designed in Le Havre, France. Today the main light is located in a nearby new tower and the old tower houses the reserve light.

Description: Cylindrical metal tower with supporting pillars, gallery and lantern room. The energy source is the diesel generator. The light is automated and connected to the monitoring system.

Finland

History

The Finnish Lighthouse Service was established in 1696 as part of the Swedish Lighthouse Service. The first lighthouse was built on the island of Utö in 1753, the second one at Porkkala in 1800.

In 1809 Finland became a Grand Duchy of the Russian Empire, and gradually a network of lighthouses emerged. Eighteen lighthouses were built in the latter part of the century alone. By World War I there were 24 lighthouses and 13 lightships, staffed by 261 persons.

The Finnish Maritime Administration was founded in 1917, soon after Finland gained independence. Its Pilotage and Lighthouse Department took charge of the maintenance of lighthouses. In the 1950s it was decide to replace all lightships with seabed lighthouses. These are fully automated lighthouses designed for Arctic conditions and capable of withstanding the pressure of moving ice fields. Today all lighthouses in Finland are unmanned. The keepers left the last manned lighthouse, Noorskär, in 1984. The last lightship was taken out of service in 1974.

Today the Hydrography and Waterways Department and FMA's district organization are responsible for the lighthouse service. At present 49 lighthouses and some 2,500 minor aids to navigation are in operation.

BENGTSKÄR LIGHTHOUSE

Geographical Position:
Latitude 59°43'40" N
Longitude 22°30'10" E
Gulf of Finland
Commissioned: 1906
Architect/Builder: Florentin Granholm / Ernst Andersin
Construction Material: Brick and stone
Tower Height: 48 meters
Focal Plane Height: 51 meters

General: This is the highest light tower in the northern Baltic. It was damaged in both world wars. In the 1930s the keepers' quarters housed up to 37 persons. Today there is a lighthouse museum, rooms for visitors, and a chapel.
Description: A three-story brick building with a round light tower of reddish granite quarried on site. Fixed, electrically powered lens. Light intensity reduced to 5,000 candelas. Light range 10.5 nautical miles, light character 2 flashes every 20 seconds.

UTÖ LIGHTHOUSE

Geographical Position:
Latitude 59°46'90" N
Longitude 21°22'30" E
North Baltic Sea
Commissioned: 1753, restored in 1814
Architect/Builder: Carl Hårleman / Robert Fithie and Kristian Trapp
Construction Material: Stone
Tower Height: 24 meters
Focal Plane Height: 40 meters

General: It is the oldest lighthouse in Finland. It was destroyed in the war of 1809 and restored in 1814. In the tower there is a chapel from the early 18th century.
Description: A 24-meter-high square masonry tower, built of stone quarried on site. The left-hand sides of the three walls facing the sea are painted white, the right-hand sides red. The fourth wall is white. Electrically powered revolving lens. The optic produces 2 flashes of 1,000,000 candelas every 12 seconds. Light range 26.5 nautical miles.

France

The French Lighthouse Service

In early times, the responsibility for building lighthouses in France was given to individual people specifically chosen for that purpose, and therefore allowed to raise light dues. The French revolution decided to suppress all light dues, and the construction of new lighthouses became the responsibility of the state.

A law, established on September 15, 1792, shared the responsibility for lighthouses between two ministeries: Interior for the construction and Marine for their maintenance.

Today, the 1,300 people working for the French Lighthouses Service belong to the Ministry of Equipment, Housing and Transportation, Department for Maritime Affairs and Mariners.

The oldest mission of the French Lighthouse Service is to manage the maritime aids to navigation along the 5,500 km French coastline, and covers:

• strategic orientations for maritime and inland waterways aids;

• relationship with users, foreign countries and international organizations;

• definition, construction and maintenance of the aids to navigation systems all over the French territories;

• maintenance of the different materials used for fighting accidental maritime oil pollutions.

More than 8,000 aids to navigation already exist, and the French Lighthouse Service is currently developing six DGPS stations along the coastline as a further improvement in the service given to mariners.

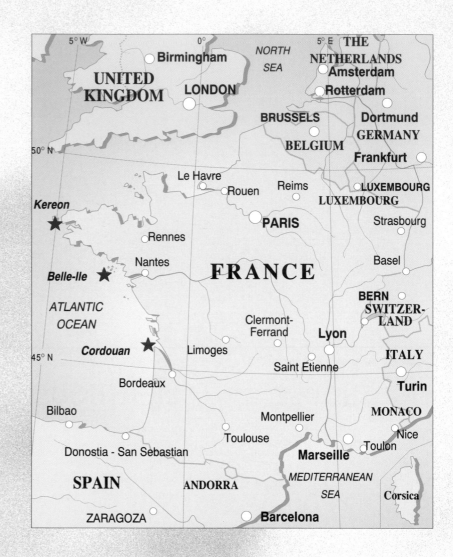

AMÉDÉE LIGHTHOUSE

Geographical Position:
Latitude 22°28'80" S
Longitude 166°27'90" E
Commissioned: 1865
Architect/Builder: Léonce Reynaud / M. Rigolet
Building Material: Iron
Tower Height: 55 meters

History: When Mr. Saisset became governor of New Caledonia in 1859, he immediatly undertook the construction of a tall lighthouse in Noumea Harbor.

In 1861 the French Lighthouse Commission proposed the construction of a major lighthouse located on Amedee Island. This proposal was approved by Sir Chasseloup Laubat, Minister for Marine and the Colonies. Leonce Reynaud prepared the drawings and Mr. Rigolet was in charge of the construction.

The main idea was to build an iron lighthouse totally prefabricated and bolted. It was first assembled and displayed in Paris, la Villette, where it was visited by many Parisians.

It was then unbolted, crated and sent to Toulon to be loaded on the vessel *Emile Pereire* under Mr. Emile Bertin's supervision. The Amedee lighthouse was erected very quickly. The work started on January 18, 1865, and the light was lit in the same year on November 15.

Description: This first-order lighthouse covers the Boulari channel, southwest of Noumea Harbor. From 1865 to 1952 it was lit with colza burners; petroleum vapor was used until 1985. It was electrified and automated using wind generators between 1985 and 1994 and photovoltaic modules after 1994.

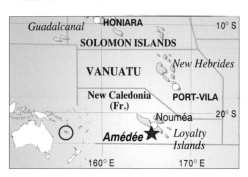

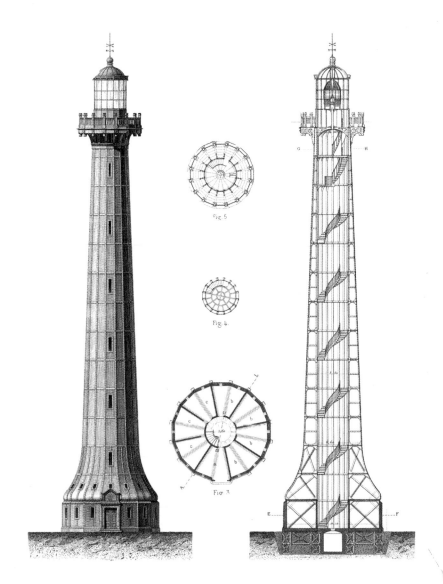

GRAND PHARE DE BELLE-ILE
(GOULPHAR)

Geographical Position:
Latitude 47°18'40" N
Longitude 03°13'39" W
Commissioned: 1835
Architect/Builder: Beautemps Beaupré,
Augustin Fresnel

Building Material: Granite
Tower Height: 52.25 meters

History: During the first half of the 10th century, mariners lobbied for the construction of a number of lighthouses.

The erection of a lighthouse on Belle-Ile island was strongly supported. It was considered one of the most important landfall sites on the French coast of the Atlantic Ocean.

The first proposal for a lighthouse was put forward in 1789. In 1820, engineer Beautemps Beaupré visited the island. A new proposal was then drawn up in early 1825. It was and presented to the French Lighthouse Commission on March 7, 1825. It was slightly modified by Augustin Fresnel. This project was approved on September 9, 1825. Unfortunately, he died before the lighthouse was erected.

It was a rather modern project, including the new concept of open stairs. During the construction, the engineers in charge of the building decided to reinforce the structure by adding a wall inside the tower. The work was partially stopped by the 1830 revolution and the lighthouse was finally finished in 1835. The official opening took place on the first of January 1836.

Description: The total height of the tower is 52.25 meters above ground, and 92.25 meters above sea level. A double lens rotating optic, with 300 mm focal length, was installed in 1903, with two metal halogen bulbs, each 1,000 watts, producing two light beams, one flash every 10 seconds, range 24 nautical miles.

The initial light used petroleum vapor; it was electrified in 1891. The radio beacon and fog horn were discontinued in 1987.

CORDOUAN LIGHTHOUSE

Geographical Position:
Latitude 45°35'11" N
Longitude 01°10'25" W
Commissioned: 1611
Architect: Louis de Foix (1584),
François Beuscher (1611),
Joseph Teulère (1789)
Building Material: Ashlar stone
Tower Height: 67.5 meters
Focal Plane Height: 43 meters

History: In 1092, monks burned a light on Cordouan Island, at the entrance of Gironde estuary, southwest of France. The first known tower was erected in 1355, at the instigation of the Prince of Wales, the Governor of Guyenne.

In 1584 Henri III asked the architect/engineer Louis de Foix to build a new tower in place of the old, which was in a state of ruin. This building was completed in 1611 by François Beuscher (Louis de Foix died during the period). The tower was extended in 1789 and 5 keepers' rooms were built around the lighthouse's basement.

The first Fresnel lens was installed at Cordouan lighthouse in 1823. The range was 21 nautical miles.

Below the tower, vaulted cellars were included for storage and water tanks were constructed to collect rainwater falling on the tower.

The lighthouse was registered as a historic monument in 1862. It is still staffed.

Description: Cordouan lighthouse is a masonry and ashlar tronconic tower, built on a 41-meter diameter basement, surrounded by a 8.5-meter high wall. Buildings and facilities are built on the basement, inside the wall: storage room, workshop, keepers' rooms, kitchen and desk office. The main access to the lighthouse is dug in the basement, closed by a thick oak door.

At the bottom of the external wall, in front of the main entrance is a 260-meter-long stone pier.

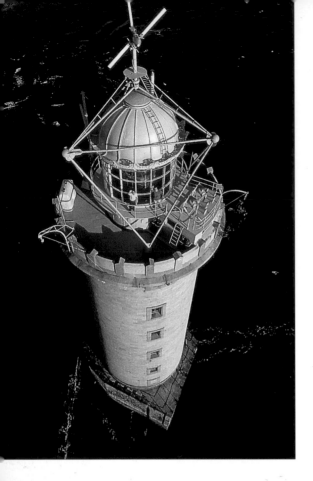

KEREON LIGHTHOUSE

Geographical Position:
Latitude 48°26'30" N
Longitude 05°01'45" W
Building period: 1907-1916
Building Material: Ashlar stone
Tower Height: 47.25 meters
above ground level; 44 meters above sea
level at maximum high tide

History: In June 1907 the French Lighthouse Commission approved the construction of a lighthouse with an oval section on the MenTensel reef, which means "aggressive stone" in the Gaelic language, at the southeast side of Ouessant Island. Building began after more than two years of preparation. It was built in an area with a very high tidal current, making the loading of materials very dangerous.

The name of the lighthouse came from a marine officer who was guillotined during the revolution and whose descendant wanted to honor his memory. In return she paid for the construction of the tower.

Ministerial approval was given and the construction began in January 1910. The lighthouse became operational in 1916.

Description: Some parts of the Kereon lighthouse were specially decorated. The staircase enclosure is covered with mosaïc. The honor room at the fifth level is the most impressive. Walls are paneled in Hungarian oak with the French Lighthouse Service logo laid on. The parquet floor in the center has an ebony and mahogany compass card inlaid into it.

The station technical equipment is run from a wind powered generator installed above the lantern. The character of the light is flashing every 24 seconds and includes red and white sectors. The nominal range is 17 nautical miles.

This offshore lighthouse is staffed and there are no plans to unstaff it. The relief is still carried out from a servicing boat, keepers move from boat to lighthouse on a balloon powered from a cable way. The relief is highly dependent on weather and sea conditions, which are bad in this area.

POINTE PLATE LIGHTHOUSE

Geographical Position:
Latitude 46°49'22" N
Longitude 56°24'10" W
West-Southwest coast of Langalde Island
Building period: 1878-1883
Architect/Builder: Albert Dolisie
Building Material: Iron
Tower Height: 43 meters

History: On May 21, 1874, the English vessel *Niobe* was wrecked on White Cape, Miquelon Island, with 153 people on board. The English government petitioned strongly to the French government for two lighthouses to be built in this very difficult English traffic area.

The French government decided, in 1882, to build two lighthouses, one of them at Pointe Plate. Sir Dolisie was in charge of this project. The lighthouse was erected on Langlade Island's cape, with maritime access only.

Originally the iron structure was composed of a central tower with three reinforcing legs. Cables complete the rigidity. Five lighthouse keepers, housed in three wooden buildings, maintain the lighthouse.

Description: The light was first produced using oil lamps, then later a petroleum vapor burner. In 1950 the lighthouse was electrified, and the building reinforced by cladding the tower and the legs in concrete. In 1967 the lighthouse was automated and de-staffed. A gas light was provided. In 1986 a wind generator replaced the gas, using an 80 watt lamp. In 1996, remote control was installed.

The beam is mainly white, except for a red sector crossing the red sector of Cap Blanc lighthouse, 13 nautical miles off the station.

The Fresnel lens was built in 1883.

Greece

Hellenic Lighthouse Service

The exact history of the Lighthouse Service is unknown, nor is the level of dependence the Service had on other authorities immediately after the gaining of Greek independence which followed the 1821 revolution against Turkish rule.

The mission of the Hellenic Lighthouse Service has always been the establishment, and provision of a lighthouse network for the country.

With the establishment of the Hellenic Lighthouse Service, a great effort was made by the new Greek State in the lighting of Greek coasts which until then were unlit. The nautical tradition of Greeks played a major part in this effort.

The first Greek beacon to be lit was at the port of Aegina in 1829. In 1831 the beacons at Port Agios Nikolaos of Kea Island and at the 3 entrances of Spetches Island were lit. In 1865 the lighthouse network had 14 beacons; in 1882, 40 beacons; in 1897, 97 beacons; and in 1912 it had 149 beacons. In the years which followed, the lighthouse network developed significantly, and in 1940 there were 388 beacons, of which 206 were manned.

After World War II new development began for the lighthouse network, and in 1995 there were 500 beacons. Today the lighthouse network has 1,190 beacons in service, with electrical energy, solar energy and acetylene gas as power sources.

GOUROUNI LIGHTHOUSE

Geographical Position:
Latitude 37°56'07" N
Longitude 23°35'07" E
West Aegean Sea
Commissioned: 1884
Construction Material: Masonry
Tower Height: 17.8 meters
Focal Plane Height: 69 meters

General: An important lighthouse of the Hellenic Lighthouse Service, it is situated on the northwest point of the island of Scopelos in order to facilitate the passage of ships through the channel between it and south Sciathos.
The building has been declared a historical monument by the Hellenic Ministry of Culture.

Description: Circular masonry tower built on a stone building. The optic produces 3 flashes of 150,000 candelas every 30 seconds.
Electricity is supplied by the national electricity network.

PLAKA LIMNOS ISLAND LIGHTHOUSE

Geographical Position:
Latitude 40°02'02" N
Longitude 25°26'08" E
North East Aegean Sea
Commissioned: 1912
Construction Material: Stone
Tower Height: 21 meters
Focal Plane Height: 55 meters

General: One of the most important lighthouses of the Hellenic Lighthouse Service, it is on the northwest point of the island of Lemnos in order to facilitate the passage of ships to and from Hellespont (Dardanelles). The lighthouse is also used for transmitting and receiving shipping and meteorological information.
Description: Circular masonry tower, 21 meters high, built in a stone building. The lighthouse uses modern lighting equipment which produces 3 flashes of 300,000 candelas every 30 seconds.
Electricity is supplied by the national electricity network. The old diesel lighting equipment is kept in the lighthouse.

PSATHOURA ALONNISOS LIGHTHOUSE

Geographical Position:
Latitude 39°30'03" N
Longitude 24°10'09" E
North Aegean Sea
Commissioned: 1895
Construction Material: Masonry
Tower Height: 17.8 meters
Focal Plane Height: 41 meters

General: This is a lighthouse with the highest tower in the Hellenic Lighthouse Service. It is very important to navigation because it covers a large area in the northern Aegean. The sea area around this islet has been nominated as a seapark for the protection of the Mediterranean seal.

Description: A circular masonry 17.8 meters tower, built on a square masonry building. The lighthouse has a modern lighting equipment FA-251 DC, which has a focal range of 17 nautical miles and flashes once every 10 seconds. Electricity is produced by solar generators. The old diesel equipment is maintained inside the lighthouse.

PSITTALIA LIGHTHOUSE

Geographical Position:
Latitude 37°56'07" N
Longitude 23°35'07" E
Saronic Gulf
Commissioned: 1856
Construction Material: Stone rubble
Tower Height: 14 meters
Focal Plane Height: 47 meters

General: This is one of the first lighthouses of the Hellenic state, and it is on the island of Psittalia in the Saronic Gulf. It was built with the aim of facilitating the approach of ships to the largest port of the country, Piraeus.

Psittalia Island has a history of over 2,000 years due to the sea battle in 480 B.C. between the Hellenic and the Persian fleets. Near the lighthouse is a monument to those who died in the battle.

Description: A 14-meter circular masonry tower is built on a square stone building. The optic produces 2 flashes of 900,000 candelas every 15 seconds.

SAPIENTZA METHONI LIGHTHOUSE

Geographical Position:
Latitude 36°44'06" N
Longitude 21°41'08" E
Northwest of Peloponnisos
Commissioned: 1885
Construction Material: Stone
Tower Height: 9.5 meters
Focal Plane Height: 116 meters

General: This is one of the most important lighthouses of the Hellenic lighthouse network since it is situated on the sea route from and to the West Mediterranean. The Sapientza islet on which the lighthouse is situated has been nominated as a national forest and it is a protected area for deer.

Description: An octagonal masonry tower, 9.5 meters high, is built on a stone building. The lighting equipment, which has modern technology with revolving lights, produces 3 flashes of 150,000 candelas every 20 seconds. Electricity is supplied by solar generators and one wind generator.

Ireland
The Commissioners of Irish Lights

The Commissioners of Irish Lights, who cover the whole of Ireland, are responsible for:
- the provision and maintenance of lighthouses and other aids to marine navigation to assist all classes of mariners in general navigation;
- sanctioning the establishment, alteration, or discontinuation of local aids to marine navigation;
- the inspection of local aids to navigation;
- marking or removing a wreck, which is a danger to navigation, where no harbor or local conservancy authority has the power to do so.

Aids to Navigation Provided

Currently the Commissioners directly maintain 80 lighthouses (which may have additional aids to navigation such as fog signals, radio beacons or radar beacons), 2 automatic lightfloats, 2 large automatic navigation buoys (Lanbys), 125 lighted and 22 unlighted buoys, 2 lighted and 17 unlighted beacons, and 2 lighted and 27 unlighted perches.

Automation and New Technology

All lighthouses operated by the Commissioners are now automated, as are the 2 lightfloats (automated lightships). Lighthouses, lightfloats and Lanbys are monitored and controlled centrally through computerized telemtery links. Lighthouses and lightfloats have part-time local attendants who carry out periodic checks and basic maintenance.

Most major offshore lighthouses are powered by electricity from diesel generating plants. Where feasible, however, wind generators or solar panels are used. Almost all lighted buoys are now solar powered.

Operational Resources

The Irish Lights Tender Granuaile is deployed to maintain the aids to navigation provided by the Commissioners. A replacement tender is planned.

A contract helicopter is used to transport maintenance personnel and materials to and from exposed offshore lighthouses.

The Commissioners' Lighthouse Depot, engineering workshops, stores, and remote control and monitoring center for lighthouses are at the Lighthouse Depot, Dun Laghoaire harbor.

Staff

The Service is currently staffed by 259 full-time administrative and technical staff, craftspeople, general operatives, and ship's officers and crew, and 80 part-time lighthouse attendants. Additional workers are employed on a casual basis as required from time to time.

Finance

The services provided by the Commissioners are financed from the General Lighthouse Fund. The income of the General Lighthouse Fund is mainly derived from light dues charged on commercial shipping at ports in Ireland and the United Kingdom, supplemented by an annual contribution from the Irish Government towards the cost of the service provided by the Commissioners in the Republic of Ireland.

FASTNET LIGHTHOUSE

Geographical Position:
Latitude 51°23'3" N
Longitude 09°36'1" W
North Atlantic Ocean
Commissioned: 1904
Architect/Builder:
William Douglass,
engineer to the
Commissioners
of Irish Lights
Construction Material:
Granite ashlar
Tower Height: 54 meters
Focal Plane Height: 49 meters

General: One of the most elegant lighthouses in the world and a monumental feat of engineering in an extremely exposed environment. The original optical apparatus, designed by C. W. Scott, engineer to the Commissioners of Irish Lights, was technically ahead of its time.

This lighthouse is well known as the turning point for the Fastnet yacht race, held every two years.

Description: A graceful gray granite tower: each stone is dovetailed into those around it, virtually bonding the structure into a monolith. The biform optic comprises 4 catadioptric panels in each tier, revolving on a mercury float. The light was converted to electric in 1969 and was automated in 1989. The electric light is in the upper tier of the optic, the lower tier now being redundant.

The light has a character of flashing white every 5 seconds. The intensity of the light is 1,823,000 candelas, giving a nominal range of 27 nautical miles. The station is also equipped with an electric horn fog signal and a racon.

HOOK HEAD LIGHTHOUSE

Geographical Position:
Latitude 52°07'3"
Longitude 06°55'7" W
Commissioned: 1172
Architect/Builder: Raymond le Gros
Construction Material: Stone rubble
Tower Height: 35 meters
Focal Plane Height: 46 meters

General: The oldest lighthouse in Ireland, and one of the oldest in the world still in operation. Thought to be the only 12th century secular building in Ireland serving its original function.

This lighthouse is situated in a designated Natural Heritage Area, an Area of Outstanding Landscape, and an Area of Landscape Importance.

Description: A massive stone tower approximately 12 meters in diameter. In the substance of the walls, which vary in thickness between 2.7 meters and 4.26 meters, are steps leading to the top of the tower. The tower is divided into three stories of vaulted construction with windows in embrasures.

The lantern was added in 1791. The present optic dates from 1911 and comprises 3 equally spaced catadioptric annular lenses floating in a mercury bath. The light was converted to electric in 1972 and automated in 1996. The character of the light is flashing white every 2 seconds. The intensity of the light is 457,000 candelas, giving a nominal range of 24 nautical miles. The station is also equipped with a horn fog signal and a racon.

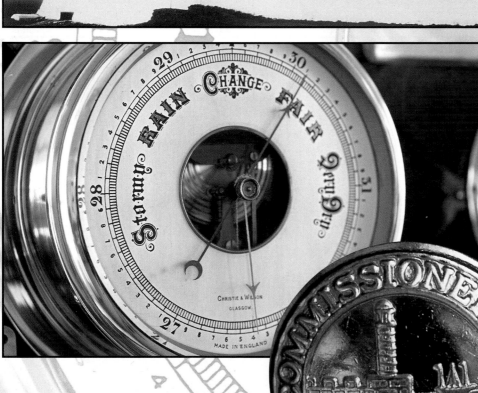

KISH LIGHTHOUSE

Geographical Position:
Latitude 53°18'7" N
Longitude 05°55'3" W
Irish Sea
Commissioned: 1965
Architect/Builder: Christiani and
Nielsen Ltd.
Construction Material: Concrete
Tower Height: 31 meters
Focal Plane Height: 29 meters

General: The first example in the world of the application of the telescopic principle to the building of a lighthouse to be placed in the open sea. This method was devised by Robert Gellerard of the Swedish Lighthouse Board but had been used only for small lighthouses in sheltered water. Kish is more than twice the size of any lighthouse of this type previously built. From 1811 to 1965 Kish Bank was marked by a lightvessel.

Description: A white concrete tower with a red band. Constructed in Dun Laghoaire Harbor as a concrete caisson 31.7 meters in diameter, and towed to its position on the Kish Bank. The caisson was then flooded and sunk onto a prepared bed of gravel. The caisson was then filled with sand and the tower was concreted to the caisson to form a monolithic structure. The light is a multicatoptric apparatus consisting of 2 faces each with 4 anodized reflectors. The light has a character of 2 white flashes every 30 seconds, and an intensity of 2,000,000 candelas which is increased to 3,000,000 candelas in fog. The nominal range is 22 miles. The station is also equipped with an electric horn fog signal.

RATHLIN WEST LIGHTHOUSE

Geographical Position:
Latitude 55°18' N
Longitude 06°16'8" W
North Channel / North Atlantic Ocean
Commissioned: 1919
Architect/Builder: Designed by
Commissioners of Irish Lights engineering
staff (Chief Engineer C. W. Scott).
Built by the Commissioners' workforce.
Construction Material: Reinforced
concrete
Tower Height: 18 meters
Focal Plane Height: 62 meters

General: A very unusual design. To avoid
the light being at too high an elevation the
lantern is at the base of the tower, giving
the impression that the the lighthouse is
upside down. The tower is built against,
and well down, a cliff face. A huge concrete
glacis is built at a 45-degree angle to the
cliff. This is an early example of a reinforced concrete lighthouse.

Description: A white concrete tower built
against the cliff face with the lantern at the
base. The optic is a first-order catadioptric
four-sided apparatus revolving on a
mercury float. The original paraffin vapor
burner was converted to electric and automated in 1983. This was the last paraffin
vapor light on the Irish coast to be converted to electric. The character of the light is
flashing red every 5 seconds. The intensity
of the light is 900,000 candelas, giving a
nominal range of 22 nautical miles.

SOUTH ROCK BEACON

Geographical Position:
Latitude 54°23'92" N
Longitude 05°24'91" W
North Atlantic Ocean
Commissioned: 1797
(light discontinued in 1877)
Architect/Builder:
Thomas Rogers
Construction Material: Granite

General: Of historical significance as this is thought to be the oldest wave-swept rock lighthouse tower in the world still standing. It was built after the first Eddystone Lighthouse (subsequently dismantled) but before Bell Rock and is the only remaining lighthouse designed and built by Thomas Rogers.

The light was discontinued in 1877 and the status of the tower reduced to that of an unlit beacon. A lightvessel was established further to the East to mark the submerged South Rock more effectively. Since then the tower has received only minimal maintenance. The lantern unfortunately was removed by thieves in 1972. The tower remains in good condition and is a remarkable tribute to the ability of Thomas Rogers as a designer and builder of lighthouses.

Italy

Il Servizio dei Fari e del Segnalamento Marittimo

The Servizio dei Fari e del Segnalamento Marittimo is responsible in Italy for approving all visual and audible fixed and floating seamarks. It maintains navigational aids of general interest in main ports, along coasts and in territorial waters. These include radio beacons and racons for a total of 57 lighthouses, 19 radio beacons, 16 racons, 25 fog signals and about 820 fixed/floating marks.

The Ministry of public works managed this service from 1860 to 1910, when the Navy took it over. While the Ministry of Public Works is still responsible for building and restoring the relevant infrastructures, all other tasks now fall to the Navy.

To carry out this task a mix of military and civilian personnel is employed in six regional commands (Marifari La Maddalena, La Spezia, Napoli, Venezia, Messina, Taranto) and one technical office (La Spezia).

The office of the Inspector (Marispefari), in Rome, is responsible for planning, direction, and control. The number of lighthouse keepers is presently undergoing reductions, following the implementation of remote control and monitoring.

Il Servizio dei Fari e del Segnalamento Marittimo

CAPO TESTA LIGHTHOUSE
SANTA TERESA DI GALLURA

Geographical Position:
Latitude 41°11'37" N
Longitude 09°08'41" E
Commissioned: 1845
Architect/Builder: Regio Ufficio del Genio Civile
Construction Material: Brick, stones
Tower Height: 23.40 meters
Focal Plane Height: 67 meters

General: Capo Testa lighthouse stands in Santa Teresa di Gallura on the Straits of Bonifacio. It was activated by Regio Ufficio del Genio Civile in 1845. The lighthouse is situated in a bound landscape district.
Description: Building on two floors surmounted by a square tower ending in cylindrical form. The lighthouse, which stands regally among the typical granitic rocks of the coast, was built with the same granitic local stones.
This construction supports a cylindric lantern house with a third-order fixed optic.
The optic produces 3 flashes of 33,000 candelas every 12 seconds and has a focal height of 67 meters. The lighthouse is powered by the national electricity network (220 volt, 50 Hz) with standby batteries.

LA LANTERNA
GENOVA

Geographical Position:
Latitude 44°24'15" N
Longitude 08°54'20" E
Commissioned: 1543
Architect/Builder: Genova Republic
Construction Material: Stones
Tower Height: 76 meters
Focal Plane Height: 117 meters

General: Genova (Genoa) lighthouse stands on the promontory of S. Benigno. The first lighthouse tower was built in 1321. Many reconstructions were necessary following bombardments during local wars. The present construction was started in March 1543 under the direction of Martino de Rosio.

Description: A 76-meter square tower built with natural stones of Carignano and Lavagna. The tower is composed of two superimposed sections with a square base; each terrace top is crowned with three series of drains. They support a cylindric lantern house with a second-order revolving optic.
The optic produces 2 flashes of 872,000 candelas every 20 seconds and has a focal height of 117 meters. This lighthouse is powered by the national electricity network (220 volt, 50 Hz) with standby batteries.
On the same site an AGA MRB-712 radio beacon transmits on 310.50 kHz at a range of 100 nautical miles.

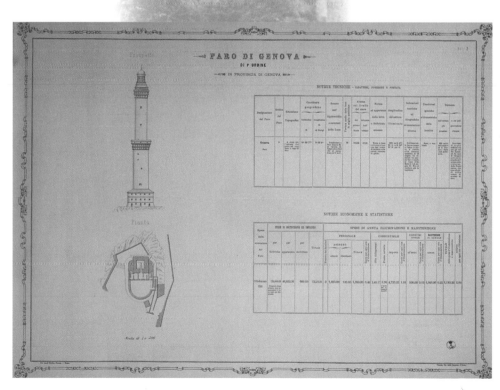

LIGHTHOUSE OF LIVORNO

Geographical Position:
Latitude 43°32'36" N
Longitude 10°17'45" E
Commissioned: 1154
Architect/Builder: Pisa Republic
Construction Material: Stone
Tower Height: 52 meters
Focal Plane Height: 52 meters

General: The first tower was built in 1154 by the Republic of Pisa. The lighthouse was destroyed by Genoan armies in 1284 and was rebuilt by the Pisa Republic in 1300. It was destroyed again during the Second World War and reconstructed with the old material in 1956 under directions of the then President of the Italian Republic, Giovanni Gronchi.

Description: A 52-meter round tower rebuilt on the old project. The tower is composed of two superimposed sections with round bases. The tower supports a white lantern house with a third-order revolving optic. The optic produces 4 flashes of 545,000 candelas every 20 seconds and has a focal height of 52 meters. This lighthouse is powered by the national electricity network (220 volt, 50Hz) with standby batteries.

On the same site an AGA MRB-712 radio beacon transmits on 298.00 kHz at a range of 100 nautical miles.

SAN RAINERI LIGHTHOUSE
MESSINA

Geographical Position:
Latitude 38°11'32" N
Longitude 15°34'33" E
Commissioned: 1857
Architect/Builder: Regio Ufficio del Genio Civile
Construction Material: Brick and stone
Tower Height: 42 meters
Focal Plane Height: 41 meters

General: This lighthouse was activated by Regio Ufficio del Genio Civile in 1857. It underwent many alterations in 1887 and in 1902 by Regio Ufficio del Genio Civile.

Description: San Raineri lighthouse is situated in the middle of a spit in the vicinity of the harbor of Messina. The tower is painted in black and white stripes and supports a cylindric lantern house with a fourth-order fixed optic. The optic produces 3 flashes of 26,000 candelas every 15 seconds and has a focal height of 41 meters. This lighthouse is powered by the national electricity network (220 volt, 50 Hz) with standby batteries.

LA ROCHETTA LIGHTHOUSE
VENEZIA

Geographical Position:
Latitude 45°20'20" N
Longitude 12°18'45" E
Commissioned: 1850
Architect/Builder: Regio Ufficio del Genio Civile
Construction Material: Brick
Tower Height: 23 meters
Focal Plane Height: 25 meters

General: The Venezia (Venice) lighthouse was activated by Regio Ufficio del Genio Civile in 1879. The tower dominates the approaches of Venezia from the sea.

Description: Unique example of an Italian lighthouse with a tower emerging from the middle of the roof. It was built entirely of bricks over a four-pitched roof.

This construction supports a cylindric lantern house with a fourth-order fixed optic. The optic produces 3 flashes of 23,400 candelas every 12 seconds and has a focal height of 25 meters. The lighthouse is powered by the national electricity network (220 volt, 50Hz) with standby batteries.

Norway

The Norwegian Lighthouse Service

While seamarks have been known from the time of the Vikings, the first lighthouse in Norway was not established until 1655, when a small wooden tower was erected at Lindesnes, at the southernmost tip of Norway. By 1700 the country did not have more than three lighthouses. In the following century, however, the development went very rapidly. By 1900 the number had increased to 162 and in 1932, when the last manned lighthouse was built, it had reached 209. This development was a tremendous financial effort for a small country with limited resources. Today 109 of the old lighthouses are still in use. They are fully automated, but 31 have a resident staff.

The lighthouses of Norway are considered an important part of the nation's heritage. In 1995 the Directorate for Cultural Heritage consequently presented a national preservation plan for the lighthouses. This plan, which is a result of a close collaboration between the maritime and the heritage authorities, has designated 84 lighthouses and five fogbell stations for preservation. Among these the two lighthouse types that are typical for Norway — the small, wooden lighthouse and the tall, elegant cast iron tower — are well represented.

The lighthouse service today is managed by the Coast Directorate in Oslo and the regional offices in the 5 coastal districts.

FÆRDER LIGHTHOUSE

Geographical Position:
Latitude 59°01'6" N
Longitude 10°31'7" E
Oslo fjord
Commissioned: 1857 (1697)
Construction Material: Cast iron

Description: The first coal-fired light was lit on the island of Store Færder in 1697 as Norway's second lighthouse. In 1857 the station was moved to Lille Færder, an island nearby, where it still stands. It was the third cast iron tower built in Norway and it is still the tallest iron tower, with its 43 meters. Apart from the tower the lighthouse consists of 8 wooden buildings, the remains of 2 earlier buildings, 2 wells, a garden, roads, 2 landings, meteorological equipment and remains of German fortifications from the Second World War. It is a very important lighthouse at the entrance of the Oslo fjord and a fine example of one of Norway's 41 cast iron towers.

GRØNNINGEN LIGHTHOUSE

Geographical Position:
Latitude 58°04'8" N
Longitude 08°05'6" E
Skagerrak
Commissioned: 1878
Construction Material: Concrete
Tower Height: 14 meters

Description: In 1878, the lighthouse service was quick to put new building materials in use. When Grønningen lighthouse was built it was one of the first dwellings in the country to be made from concrete. The form is clearly influenced by contemporary military and industrial architecture. Electricity was installed in the lighthouse in 1960. It was automated and unmanned in 1980. Today the dwellings are used for cultural purposes. The lighthouse was listed in 1994 as a historical monument under the Cultural Heritage Act.

HOMLUNGEN LIGHTHOUSE

Geographical Position:
Latitude 59°00'9" N
Longitude 11°01'9" E
Oslo fjord
Commissioned: 1867
Construction Material: Wood

Description: This small wooden lighthouse was built in 1867 on the archipelago of Hvaler, on the west side of the Oslo fjord. The lighthouse was rebuilt in 1915, and since then little has been changed. The lighthouse station thus appears in a very authentic shape. Homlungen was automated in 1952 and serves, in addition to its original use, as a holiday spot for the Coast Directorate. The lighthouse and the nearby fishing village of Lauer are important parts of the historical landscape. Homlungen lighthouse is also a very good example of a typical Norwegian wooden lighthouse.

KVITSØY LIGHTHOUSE

Geographical Position:
Latitude 59°03'8" N
Longitude 05°24'1" E
North Sea
Commissioned: 1700
Construction Material:
Stone/brick
Tower Height: 27 meters

Description: In 1700 a Royal permission was granted to establish a light at Kvitsøy. The first construction was a lever light with a coal-basket. The light was not a great financial success for the owner, who nevertheless was named von Fyhren (*fyhr* in Norwegian means lighthouse). In 1815 the lighthouse was taken over by the government, and in 1829, an 18 meter high hexagonal stone tower was erected. In 1859 the tower was heightened to 27 meters and the coal-basket was replaced by an oil burner. Electricity was installed in the lighthouse in 1939. It was later automated and unmanned in 1969. Kvitøy is the only lighthouse in Norway where the old coal-fire tower is still in use.

The lighthouse will be listed as a historical monument under the Cultural Heritage Act.

LINDESNES LIGHTHOUSE

Geographical Position:
Latitude 57°59'0" N
Longitude 07°02" E
North Sea
Commissioned: 1655
Construction Material: Stone (ruin), cast iron

Description: At the very southern point of Norway, the first lighthouse in the country was erected in 1655. It was a wooden tower of unknown construction. Later a lever light was put up, and in 1799 the first stone tower was built. At the same time a twin light was put up at Markøy, an island nearby. In 1822 the tower was renewed and the coal fire was surrounded by a glass and iron dome. The present iron tower was erected in 1915, a few meters away from the stone tower that still exists without its dome. During the Second World War the lighthouse was occupied by the Germans. Today their fortifications are a part of the station's history. Plans for a National Lighthouse Museum at Lindesnes have recently been put forward.

Poland

Polish Lighthouse
Service

Prior to 1920 there was no uniform system for management of lighthouse service in Poland. The first steps taken in this direction were made by the Naval Hydrographic Office. Under them the Civilian Maritime Administration was established in 1926. Duties of administering the lighthouse service were given to the Service of Aids to Navigation (SAN).

Between the years 1926 to 1936, Masters Offices were set up in Hel, Puck and Gdynia. These offices managed and modernized lighthouses and additional aids to navigation. After World War II the activities of SAN increased as it engaged in reconstruction of destroyed lighthouses. In the 1940s, 10 lighthouses were put back into operation.

In 1991 a reorganization occured in which a new office was created outside of the Maritime Office for a period of four years. The new office was the Hydrographic Office of the Republic of Poland who was responsible for the process of reforms in maritime administration completed in 1995. This incorporated the Hydrographic Office into the Maritime Offices in Gdynia and Szczecin, creating the Aids to Navigation Departments. At present, these two departments are responsible for the aids to navigation operating along the 500 km coastline. The deployment of maritime transport in conjunction with international assistance from IALA and IMO has helped in constantly improving aids to navigation.

ROZEWIE LIGHTHOUSE (CAPE)

Geographical Position:
Latitude 54°49'54" N
Longitude 18°20'20" E
South coastline of Baltic Sea
Commissioned: November 15, 1822
(replacement of lighthouse which existed in 1696)
Construction Material:
Stones, metal
Tower Height: 32.2 meters
Focal Plane Height: 83.2 meters

General: This is one of the oldest lighthouses on the Baltic Sea. It can be found on Swedish charts from 1696. This lighthouse was declared a National Monument on January 4, 1972. Rozewie Cape is the northernmost point of Poland.

Description: The 20-meter metal tower, painted red, is situated on a 13-meter circular cone base.
The lighthouse optic has been changed twice. Presently, the lantern house accommodates the main and standby light sources, and a revolving pedestal. The optic produces a flash of 1,800,000 candelas. Electricity is supplied by the national electricity network with an auxiliary generator. This site also contains a nautophone-type fog signal and DGPS reference station.
The lighthouse and buildings are a harmonized construction, dominating Rozewie Cape and exhibiting the oldest architectural tower in the area.

NIECHORZE LIGHTHOUSE

Geographical Position:
Latitude 54°05'47" N
Longitude 15°03'57" E
South coastline of Baltic Sea
Commissioned: 1866
Construction Material: Bricks, light yellow
Tower Height: 44 meters
Focal Plane Height: 62.6 meters

General: This is one of the most beautiful lighthouses on the south coastline of the Baltic Sea.

Description: A tower built on veneered bricks, light yellow in color. The cross-section of the tower is square in shape up to a height of 13 meters. It then takes on an octagonal form. The tower ends in a strong protruding molding.
The lighthouse was equipped with a first-class Fresnel apparatus. The present source of light is a bulb placed in a revolving four-directional optical apparatus with circular lenses.
The power of the lamp is 1,000 watts and is placed in an automatic, two-position lamp changer.
In case of electricity failure, the lighthouse is supplied by electrical generator.
The building and the lighthouse are a harmonized construction, architecturally dominating the village of Niechorze.

OCE

ANIA

NEW ZEALAND P.164

Australia

Australian Aids to Navigation

Until the creation of the Australian Federation in 1901, the various colonial governments provided aids to navigation coverage within the coastal areas of their respective states. The Departments of the Commonwealth Government took on the responsibilities for the design, construction, operation, and maintenance of Australia's coastal lighthouses from 1915 to 1991. In 1991 these duties were taken over by the Australian Maritime Safety Authority. Functions of the Authority include ship survey and seafarer qualifications, coordination of Australian search and rescue, and national and international marine pollution issues. The State and Territory administrations still control lights that are used within port limits and inland waterways.

The Authority has responsibility for some 400 aids to navigation including beacons, lights, lightvessels, racons, and DGPS broadcasting stations, all of which cover approximately 37,000 km of coastline. These aids to navigation are funded by the shipping industry and are serviced by road, helicopter, or the Authority's 75.4 meter lighthouse tender MV Cape Grafton.

Light sources vary and are generally of a nature consistent with current technological advances. As of 1997 aids were powered by electricity and solar power.

Over 120 of the Australian Maritime Safety Authority's lighthouse buildings date back to the 19th century and the majority are on the (heritage) Register of the National Estate.

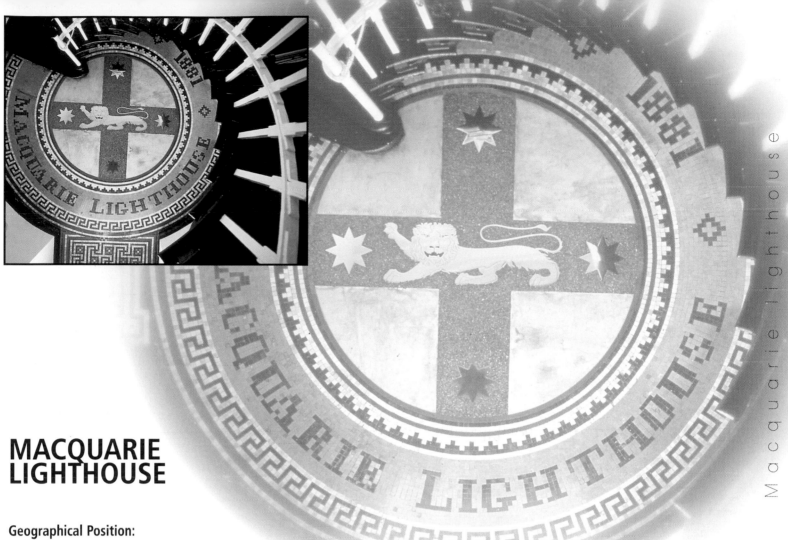

MACQUARIE LIGHTHOUSE

Geographical Position:
Latitude 33°51'3" S
Longitude 151°17' E
Commissioned: 1817
Original tower: Francis Greenaway
Existing tower: James Barnett
Construction Material: Sandstone
Tower Height: 24 meters
Focal Plane Height: 105 meters

General: The existing tower is on the site of the original woodburning aid to navigation. The tower design is an adaptation of the convict architect-designed first tower. The site is the most historically significant lighthouse site in Australia. The light-station was included in the Register of National Estate in the 1970s.

Description: An 18.5-meter round masonry tower rising from a rectangular pavilion with ornamental domes. It supports a white Chance Bros. lantern house with a fourth-order double flashing revolving optic. The optic produces two flashes of 800,000 candelas intensity each 10 seconds and has a focal plane height of 106 meters. Power is supplied from the city's electricity supply and a standby diesel generator is available. Two sectors are provided within Sydney Harbor to assist vessel pilotage.

New Zealand

History

The Maritime Safety Authority of New Zealand is directly responsible for coastal aids to navigation. These consist of 39 day beacons, 5 buoys, 1 light on primary battery, 2 lights on diesel generators, 24 lights on national electricity network power, and 68 lights on solar power. Most lights are light-beacons, only 23 being classic lighthouses. All lights are completely automatic and the major lights are monitored by computer. Aids to navigation inside harbor limits are administered by local authorities. There are no lighthouse keepers.

The Maritime Safety Authority's aids to navigation are maintained by private contractors. Any upgrades or major works, including repainting of classic lighthouses, are subject to competitive public tender. Private consultants are used as necessary to manage major works.

The Maritime Safety Authority Lighthouse Division has a staff of one Lighthouse Engineer who manages all aspects of the service. The Maritime Safety Authority owns a four-wheel-drive utility vehicle for use during the Lighthouse Engineer's inspections, and hires helicopters and boats when necessary.

The Maritime Safety Authority of New Zealand reports to the Minister of Transport and is funded by the Government. A marine safety charge is levied on all commercial vessels over 8 meters in length.

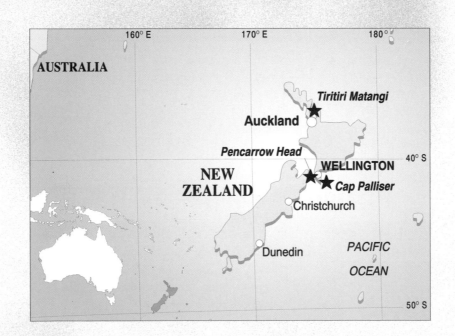

CAP PALLISER LIGHTHOUSE

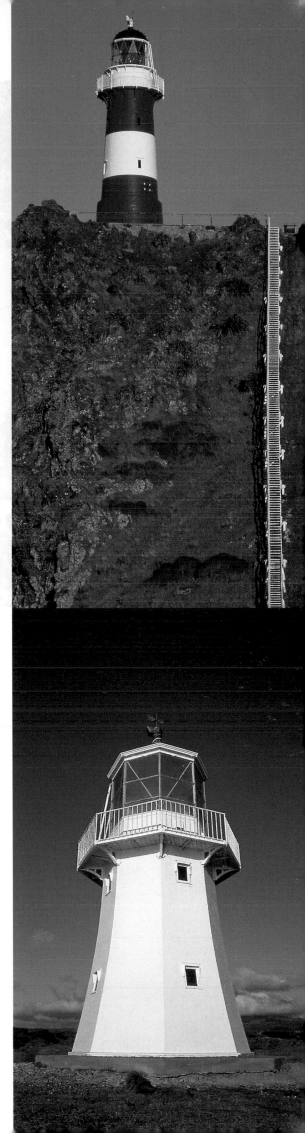

Geographical Position:
Latitude 41°37' S
Longitude 175°17' E
Commissioned: 1897
Construction Material: Cast iron
Tower Height: 18 meters
Focal Plane Height: 78 meters

General: This is a red and white tower, made in England. Cast iron sections are bolted together and sit on a concrete base. Second-order revolving lenses flash twice every 20 seconds. It has a range of 26 nautical miles, and was lit for the first time on October 27, 1897. The light was converted from oil and kerosene to diesel generated electricity in 1954. It was eventually connected to the national electricity network in 1967, with an automatic standby diesel generator. The lighthouse keepers were withdrawn in 1986. The operation of the light is now monitored by a computer.

PENCARROW HEAD LIGHTHOUSE

Geographical Position:
Latitude 41°21'7" S
Longitude 174°51' E
Commissioned: 1859
Construction Material: Cast iron
Tower Height: 10 meters
Focal Plane Height: 98 meters

General: This is a white tower, made in England of cast iron sections bolted together. The light, 98 meters above sea level, was first lit on January 1, 1859. It was the first permanent light to be built in New Zealand, and the only light in New Zealand ever to have a woman keeper. The light is a second-order catadioptric, with eclipses at intervals of 2 minutes, and visible for 26 nautical miles. It was decommissioned in 1935 and is now officially designated a historic place.

TIRITIRI MATANGI ISLAND LIGHTHOUSE

Geographical Position:
Latitude 36°36' S
Longitude 174°54' E
Commissioned: 1865
Construction Material: Cast iron
Tower Height: 20 meters
Focal Plane Height: 91 meters

General: This is a white tower, made in England of cast iron sections bolted together. The light, 91 meters above sea level, was first lit on January 1, 1865. It was converted from oil illumination to acetylene gas in 1925, and to diesel generated electricity in 1955. A xenon lamp producing 10 million candelas was fitted in 1956, making it one of the most powerful lights in the world at that time. It was connected to the national electricity network via a 5 km underwater cable in 1966. In 1984 the lighthouse keepers were withdrawn. The present light is powered by

solar panels connected to a battery that powers the light at night. It flashes once every 15 seconds and has a range of 18 nautical miles.

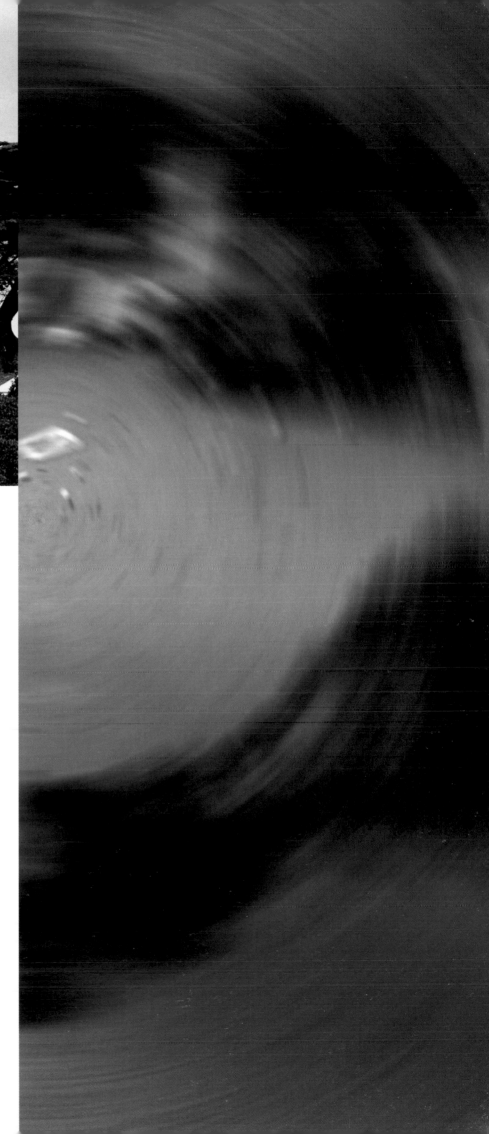

Table of

PREFACE

INTRODUCTION

AFRICA

AMERICA

ASIA

Contents

PHOTOGRAPH CREDITS

Jean Guichard: pages 8, 13 bottom left, 14 bottom left, 15, 16 top, 16 bottom left and bottom right,
17 left, 130, 132, 134, 135, 136, 137, 138, 144, 145, 149 top, 170-171.
Calbrix: page 139. Y. Skoulas: pages 141, 142, 143. H. Bancaud: page 79 top. Z. Grabowiecki: page 159
A.-V. Oeveren: pages 42, 43. E.-H. Irwin: page 45. A.-C. Diaz: pages 50, 51. Trinity House: page 106 top right.
Shell Mex BP News: page 105. Daily Mail: page 104 middle left. National archives, photography service: pages 27, 28, 29, 30 and 31.
Grant Sheehan photography: page 166.

Repro-house: Nord Compo, Villeneuve d'Ascq (59), France
Cartography: Patrick Mérienne
Graphic design: Laurence Morvan

© 1998, by The Globe Pequot Press, Old Saybrook
First edition: © 1998, Edilarge S.A. Editions Ouest-France, Rennes, France
French title: Phares du Monde
Printed by Pollina, Luçon (85), France - n° 75636
ISBN 0-7627-0387-3
Library of Congress cataloging-in-Publication data is available.